CU00894795

HIDDEN GARDENS OF SPAIN

EDUARDO MENCOS

FRANCES LINCOLN

EDUARDO MENCOS

HIDDEN GARDENS OF SPAIN

To my grandmother, Teresa Ozores, Marquesa de Casa Valdés, who sowed the seed.
And to my wife Anneli Bojstad, who brought it to fruition.

Frances Lincoln Ltd
4 Torriano Mews
Torriano Avenue
London NW5 2RZ
www.franceslincoln.com

Hidden Gardens of Spain

Copyright © Frances Lincoln Ltd 2004
Text and photographs copyright © Eduardo Mencos 2004

First Frances Lincoln edition: 2004

Eduardo Mencos has asserted his right to be identified as the author of this work in accordance with the Copyright, Designs and Patents Act 1988 (UK).

All rights reserved. No part of this publication may be reproduced, stored in a retrieval system or transmitted in any form, or by any means, electronic, mechanical, photocopying, recording or otherwise, without either permission in writing from the publisher or a licence permitting restricted copying. In the United Kingdom such licences are issued by the Copyright Licensing Agency, 90 Tottenham Court Road, London W1T 4LP.

A catalogue record for this book is available from the British Library.

ISBN 0 7112 1964 8

Printed and bound in Singapore

1 2 3 4 5 6 7 8 9

ACKNOWLEDGMENTS

Writing this book has been a long journey and it has been delightful to deepen my knowledge of Spain on the way. But what makes me even more grateful is that I have met the Spanish gardeners within these pages. Many gave me board and lodgings as well as conversation, sharing the living adventure of their gardens and the insights they have been granted.

Special thanks to the kind and masterly Leandro and Julia Silva, to the vital and enthusiastic Duke of Segorbe, to the Veals for their limitless hospitality in London, to Jo Christian and Andrew Dunn for their British humour and support in the journey towards publication and of course to my wife Anneli, for driving me on in pursuit of excellence. I cherish my memories of happy moments and shared gardening tales with the following people, to all of whom my thanks:

Maribel Aguirre de Úrcola; Isabel Aguirre de Úrcola; Duquesa de Alba; Maribel Aldasoro; Charo Andrade; Marqueses de Aranda; Inés Argüelles; Jacobo Argüelles; Juan Alberto Arnús; Lourdes Arroyo; Sres de Babé; Duques de Bailén; Goli Bahktiar; Sofía Barroso; José Felipe Beltrán; Juan-José Benítez de Lugo; Ana María Bergarajauregui; Adela Bermúdez; Conde de Bugallal; Sres de Caballero de Luján; Jesús Miguel Cabrera; Antonio Cabrero; Marqueses de Campo Real; Marqueses de Canillejas; Rosalía Cavanilles; María Jesús Cagiga; Ana Campón; Pío Caro-Baroja; Sres de Carter; Alfonso Carvajal; Isabel Carvajal; Mercedes del Castillo; María del Carmen Castillo-Olivares; Manuel Claudel; Sres de Coleridge; María Teresa Collantes; Xavier Corberó; Martín Chirino; Alberto Delclaux; Adolfo Domínguez; Jesús Domínguez; Sres de Erquicia; Isaac Escalante; Marqueses de la Esperanza; Condesa de Fefiñanes; María Dolores Fernández-Figares; Bet Figueras; Condesa Vda de Fontanar; Gill Ford; Antonio Galván; Ana Gamazo; Vda de García-Valdecasas; Heidi Gildemeister; Francisco González-Camino; Luis González-Camino; Lord Grigg; Marqueses de Griñón; Sres de Gruyter; Vizconde de Güell; Fernanda Guerrero; Elena Gut; Margara Haffner; Cristina Heeren; Penelope Hobhouse; Gerald Huggan; José Jimenéz Salazar; Juan von Knobloch; Fabiola Larios; Enrique Luis Larroque; Marquesa de Las Palmas; Marqueses de Legarda; Trinidad Lopera; Condesa de Los Llanos; Sres de Lozano; Marqueses de Lozoya; Marqués de Marianao; Lukas Markenie; Sres de Marchesi; Christopher Masson; Alicia Maura; Sres de Mayans; María Medina; Sres de Monjardín; Isabel Montojo; Salvador Montoro; Condes de Montseny; Kuky Mora-Figueroa; Juan Müller; Cristina Navarro; Sres de Oria; Jaime Ortiz Patiño; Beatriz de Orleáns; Sres de Ortuño; Marina Osorio; Hermanas Pan de Soraluce; Angela Parias; Sres de Parladé; Duques de Pastrana; Juan Peñalosa; Guillermo Pérez-Villalta; Duarte Pinto-Coelho; Pedro Piñeiro; Mary Pirón; Inmaculada Porras; Marqueses de Pozoblanco; Conde de Priegue; Marqués de Rafal; Sres de Real; Condesa de Revilla de Camargo; Cristina Rodríguez-Acosta; Miguel; Rodríguez-Acosta; Sres de Rodríguez-Azero; Vda. de Rodríguez-Torres; Luisa Roquero; Javier Roviralta; Barbara de Rueda; Blanca de Rueda; Marqués de San Andrés; Duque de San Carlos; Ignacio Sangro de Liniers; Marqueses de Santa Cruz de Rivadulla; Alberto Satrústegui; Luis Schneider; Sres de Sert; Sres de Shay; Sres de Soto; Sres de Stewart; Pedro Trapote; Oscar Tusquets; Sres de Ullrich; Micaela Valdés; Joaquín Vázquez; Marquesa de Viesca de la Sierra; Marqués de Villanueva de Valdueza; Sres de Winckler; Concha Ybarra; Sres de Zamacola; Alfonso Zobel; Jaime Zobel; Pedro Zubiría.

CONTENTS

PROLOGUE

There seems little point in my writing about this book, which speaks so eloquently for itself. Nor shall I write about gardening, for though I am a garden lover and a gardener, there is nothing I could usefully add to what Eduardo Mencos has set down here. The function of this prologue, as I see it, is to say a word or two about Eduardo.

I first met Eduardo in 1999, when he phoned to ask if he could come and take some pictures of our garden. We protested that the few battered shrubs and flowers that remained unravaged by our sheep hardly constituted a garden at all, let alone one that justified appearing in *Casa y Campo*, the magazine Eduardo was working for.

'I have heard about your garden,' he said, 'and I would like to come and see it. I love to see what the English do with their gardens in our country.' In the end he persuaded us . . . his charm is hard to resist.

Ana, my wife, dead-headed a rose, while I moved a pile of bricks. At the appointed hour he hurtled into the valley in a cloud of dust. He unfolded himself from his car, a boyish, blond bear of a man, and by the time we reached my home I had fallen beneath the spell of his warm smile and his rich, confident voice. I noted that he knew how to listen as well as how to tell a good story, and we quickly found a number of radical notions upon which we agreed.

We showed him sheepishly round the garden, and it was soon clear that he could see things that we were quite unaware of. He opened our eyes both to new possibilities and to the beauty of what was already there. Many of Ana's more offbeat notions, which I had hitherto dismissed as eccentric rantings, became clear with Eduardo's guidance. We were still a long way off *Casa y Campo*, but Eduardo certainly enriched my appreciation of my wife's inspirations.

There is a spiritual, even mystical side to Eduardo which shines through the pages of this book. Of course the best way to enjoy this is to walk round a garden or landscape with the man himself, and enjoy the pleasure of the company of a refined, yet exuberant, sensibility to nature. We can't all enjoy such a pleasure though; Eduardo's time is limited. *Hidden Gardens of Spain* is the next best thing.

There are countless garden books, and all, to a certain extent, represent the spirit of the age and the place they were written in. Eduardo is a wonderful Virgil to lead us into the gardens of the new century. For as well as being solidly grounded in the traditional practices of garden design, he does not fear to be iconoclastic, to break moulds and explore new ideas.

There is also a strong sensuous element in Eduardo's response to nature; he is never embarrassed to seek out the essence, the spirit and the mystery of things. Maybe this has developed through his involvement in the film industry, as producer and director of his own films. He certainly has something of a cinematographic way of looking at the world. His innovativeness was very apparent in his film-making too. He has never been one to fear going out on a limb. In fine Spanish hidalgo style, he decided that his last film should be directed entirely from horseback. This might not seem such a radical departure . . . except that most of the action of the film takes place in an apartment in Madrid.

So that's a bit of the Eduardo you won't get in the biographical notes, and if it has warmed your heart a little to this extraordinary man, and thus increased the enjoyment you get from his enchanting book, then my scribbling has been fruitful.

Chris Stewart, Granada, 23 April 2004

INTRODUCTION

The phone rings and an anxious voice at the other end says that a fire is threatening to swallow up my *finca* and my garden like some hungry dragon. For days a hot Saharan wind has enveloped Spain, pushing temperatures into the forties and covering everything with a cloud of dust. When I arrive, the sight of a calm fireman reassures me. Several trees are blackened but the fire has been stopped in time. I breathe a sigh of relief; my garden has been saved.

This is an example of how temperamental the Spanish climate can be, with its dry, torrid summers and the torrential rain and bitter cold of winter. The Iberian peninsula is like a castle whose walls are mountains – the long *cordilleras* and *sierras* – fringed by a narrow coastal plain where the sea air creates a temperate zone. In the interior is a great plateau with an average height of about 600 metres/1800 feet above sea level and a continental climate. This plain is subject to Atlantic weather fronts.

However, Spain's position between the Mediterranean and the Atlantic makes it difficult to generalize about climate. Sierra de Grazalema, for example, is the rainiest place in the country, but just a few kilometres away at Almería, also in Andalusia, is the driest spot in Europe.

Variety is also at the heart of Spanish gardening, which is a blend of many traditions. The Romans gave us the patio and the art of topiary. Eight centuries of Moorish occupation added to the Roman heritage another source of inspiration in the shape of the Persian garden. The Hispano-Arabic garden is the result of this cross-fertilization, which has brought forth some of the most refined and sublime examples of the art of garden design.

Christians and Moors fought and lived alongside one another for centuries in a medieval culture where cities such as Córdoba, Granada and Seville developed and hundreds of monasteries were founded. Both groups cultivated formal cross-shaped gardens as well as kitchen gardens.

To the Renaissance, when Spain was the foremost world power, belongs the creation of the gardens at Aranjuez and El Escorial for Philip II. At Aranjuez an old hunting lodge was transformed into an exuberant oasis in the middle of the Castilian steppe. Although the inspiration was Italian and Flemish, the garden retained its Hispanic roots: it was at once grandiose and intimate. At Escorial the garden was permitted to sweeten the severe classicism of the architecture, like a woven carpet. Later the Bourbon dynasty of Philip V commissioned the baroque gardens at La Granja. Inspired by the gardens at Versailles, the king set about creating a baroque garden where crystalline mountain streams are transformed into a fabulous spectacle. Throughout the days of the Spanish empire the kings of Spain imported trees and plants from the Americas, and the royal gardens became the antechamber for the entry of plants into the rest of Europe.

After a long period of lethargy following the Civil War, today Spanish gardening has a new vitality. Economic development has fed the popular interest in gardening. The hundreds of thousands of gardening northern Europeans who have settled in Spain have also been influential.

Why these particular gardens? The choice is subjective, of course, but I have tried to choose gardens from all over Spain, and especially those created in the last few years. Sadly, I have not been able to include anything from the Basque country. It seems that gardening is another victim of terrorism.

Exploring the hidden gardens of Spain has been an enthralling journey for me. Each of the owners would welcome me into their own little Eden and we would share an enchanted moment there. I hope that through this book I will be able to share that magic.

THE NORTH

PALACIO DE OCA

TOUCHING THE SKY

OPPOSITE: The upper of the two water tanks or pools that form the central axis of the garden, seen from the bridge that separates them. This pool is surrounded by battlements and hydrangeas, which grow to huge sizes. The tilias and box here grow to over 4 metres/ 13 feet high.

BELOW LEFT: Water from the upper pool travels down this granite pipe and gushes into the pool below.

BELOW RIGHT: An eighteenth-century fountain dominates the quadrangle outside the entrance hall of the *pazo*. The quadrangle took on its current appearance, complete with rounded box hedges, in the 1920s.

Mist, rain, green – a thousand glowing greens. Damp shade and sweet water, quickened, tender or passionate. Everything in Oca is cool and wet, like the soft Atlantic air which generously moistens Galicia and its stones, the impermeable granite of the buildings, which is wedded so harmoniously to the living architecture of trees and plants.

Oca is the finest example of the Galician country seat or *pazo*. *Pazo* derives from the Latin word *palatium*, or palace, and the *pazo* at Oca is so representative of the Galician ideal that it is accorded the distinction of being called *palacio*. In the garden, which mostly dates from the eighteenth century, the practical and the beautiful are united in a network of canals and two water tanks. The canals and water tanks form the central axis of the garden, bordered by hydrangeas and separated from each other by a narrow stone bridge covered by trained vines.

The Duke of Segorbe, who is responsible for the recent restoration of the gardens, explains the symbolism of the tanks. 'The boat on the lower tank is a warship, with cannons and mariners. We're returning the garden to its original state by planting lemon and bitter orange trees in the boat to symbolize purgatory. The boat on the upper tank is a trading ship, with merchant seamen, and the sweet orange trees planted there represent paradise.'

Oca began its voyage through the years as a fortress. During the eighteenth century Andrés Gayoso y López de Lema and his son Fernando, Marquis of Camarasa, gave it its current shape, with the refined iconography so characteristic of the Baroque period.

The adventures of the garden continued into the nineteenth century when the French designer François Viet was given the task of transforming vegetable patches into a landscape garden with winding paths. The trees planted in this period are typical of the age, including eucalyptus, cryptomeria and magnolia.

Now, like the moving, living waters that inhabit this magical place, the Duke of Segorbe and his head gardener Manuel Conde Ares – who contend with each other in passion for the garden – are investigating, restoring and bringing fresh ideas. They have added a splendid maze, modelled on the maze at Canterbury Cathedral, and a topiary crocodile.

Every time I visit I have the same sensation of time both suspended and moving, of stone and plants. And every time Manuel, the happy gardener, says with a crafty smile, 'I've got something new to show you . . .'

The show goes on!

ABOVE: The maze is the most recent addition to the garden. It is a copy of the one at Canterbury Cathedral.

LEFT: Moss and stone make this corner magical. It is surrounded by battlements recalling the origins of the castle fortress at Oca. Though Oca dates to the sixteenth century, it was in the eighteenth century that it became the glorious baroque *palacio* that we see today.

OVERLEAF: This stone warship laden with hydrangeas is a riot of flowers in July and August.

JAZ

A SUIT OF LIGHTS

The first thing a visitor to Jaz feels is astonishment at the splendid, exquisite purple garment that clings to the house like a young woman's evening gown. Bougainvillea, although originally from Brazil, has become the star of many Spanish gardens, especially on the Mediterranean coast and the Balearic Islands. It also grows in the north, thanks to the temperate climate, and without doubt the most spectacular bougainvillea in Spain is here at Jaz.

The house, which is on a hill, is like a great viewing gallery over the city of La Coruña. Although the house is built on an old *pazo*, its character was transformed during renovations in 1911 when cement was used for the first time in the area, and large windows were created to provide better communication with the outdoors. All this was done to make the house more appealing in the summer, the time when it is in use.

The garden, which dates from the same era, has a markedly French feel to its geometric layout. On the north side of the house twelve parterres planted with agapanthus bordered by trimmed box hedges all lead to a sundial standing in a small courtyard.

But the most spectacular part of the garden is that which faces the midday sun, where a yew tree is ringed by box, and a succession of parterres filled with great banks of canna lilies and the bougainvillea behind them offer an unsurpassable explosion of colour.

One of the many co-owners of Jaz comments, 'Despite the difficulties of maintaining this place with all the differences of interest and opinion among the family, we are all agreed that the garden is the priority. It will remain perfect, even at the expense of the house and its interior.'

So, contradicting the spiritual gurus, here what is on the outside is more important than what is on the inside.

RIGHT: The emphatic lines of the box hedges contrast with the rounded forms of yew, here shaped into giant 'acorns' around a lively fountain.

OVERLEAF: *Bougainvillea glabra* covers the front of the house and dominates the garden, flourishing in the temperate Galician climate. The purple contrasts with the red tones of *Canna indica* and the blue agapanthus growing among the hedges.

BELOW: Solid hedges of *Buxus sempervirens* 'Suffruticosa' define beds of delicate *Agapanthus africanus*. The paths converge on a small patio with benches and a stone sundial.

PAZO DE PEGULLAL

THE ADOPTED CHILD

There cannot be many places in Spain where Mother Nature is as kind and generous as she is in this corner of southern Galicia. There is plenty of rain here and the temperature is always mild. The climate is like that of a huge greenhouse where Mediterranean palms, cypresses and lemon trees can be grown as easily as camellias, rhododendrons and hydrangeas.

When the owners arrived here, the fact that there was no garden, let alone any trees, almost put them off for ever, but instead their enterprising spirit inspired them to accept the challenge of starting a garden from nothing. They set about planting trees, but after a time they felt lost and dissatisfied when the results did not fulfil their aspirations. When they came across photographs of a garden designed by Fernando Carruncho – then just starting out as a landscape artist – they got in touch with him. They took out the few things that they had planted, and even returned many plants that had been ordered from the nursery. This way Carruncho could design the garden without being hampered by the past.

'We agreed with him on almost everything and hardly made any changes to his plans,' the owner explains. 'But we were very influenced by our son, who wanted us to have a maze; he'd seen one in a movie and it had made a big impression on him. If it was going to be a central part of the garden, we wanted to make sure that we could see

it from the house, and that it wasn't obscured by the cloister-like pergola that we were also planning.' As we approach the ivy maze, talk turns to Stanley Kubrick's film *The Shining* and the terrifying scenes where Jack Nicholson is chasing his wife through the snowy maze with an axe.

The technical drawing and design work of the garden may have been the brainchild of someone else, but the owner speaks about her garden with all the pride of a devoted mother. It is her work in progress. She is currently planning to make the most of the autumn by planting shrubs and trees which are at their colourful best at that time of year: grapevines, liquidambar and tulip trees. It is also, she explains, her sanctuary. 'It's a sensual place, full of the kind of pleasures that money can't buy, like seeing how much my children love it here and how it has given them respect for nature. My elder son travels here to see how the wisteria, the azaleas or the magnolias are blooming.' Every flowering is a journey.

ABOVE: A mossy statue of Il Bachino – a clown figure very popular in Renaissance gardens – sits happily in a fountain.

OPPOSITE: The different levels of the garden are linked by a magnificent wisteria-covered pergola, which gives both shade and colour.

OVERLEAF: Low flowerbeds and box hedges on the terrace of the upper level contrast with the vertical lines of the cypresses beyond. Shady seats under the pergola invite the visitor to linger.

LEFT: The southern façade is reflected in a stretch of water flanked by *Hypericum calycinum*.

BELOW LEFT: A soft white carpet of *Rhododendron* 'Palestrina' is in sharp contrast with the geometric lines elsewhere in the garden.

BELOW: A maze has been created on the lower level by training ivy (*Hedera helix*) and climbing roses over metal frames. A small pavilion sits at its centre.

PAZO DE SANTA CRUZ

THE OTHER SPAIN

To foreign eyes, Spain is a bright country, bathed in sunshine. But in this region of Galicia, and especially in this garden, with its huge trees, immense box trees and many different manifestations of water, we discover a Spain of dark shadows.

The estate of Santa Cruz was founded in the sixteenth century by an ancestor of the present owner, who is Alfonson Armada, Marquis of Santa Cruz de Ribadulla. He explains that this is probably the most botanically significant garden in Galicia because of the abundance of exotic species that began to be introduced from the seventeenth century on. 'Among these we can find more than five hundred varieties of camellia,' says the Marquis, who has become an expert in the field and Spain's foremost cultivator of camellias.

However, the main attractions of the estate are the spectacular avenues of vast olives, remains of an earlier garden, which unite to form an imposing cross that could be considered the first piece of landscaping here. The avenues were created by Juan Ibánez de Mondragón, who acquired the medieval tower of Ortiguera in the sixteenth century in order to convert it into his family seat. 'The

dense, damp forest of Atlantic species grew up towards the end of the seventeenth century, and as time passes it becomes almost impossible to tell that they were planted by man,' the Marquis comments. He points out a fish pond and a waterfall marked with carved stones, the only remaining features that hint at human origins.

The garden reached its full splendour in the era of Iván Armada, the seventh Marquis who lived here from 1880 to 1899. A great botanist, he introduced nearly five thousand specimens, including *Dicksonia antarctica*, *Sequoiadendron giganteum* and *Gunnera manicata*.

The camellia is queen in this garden, lighting up the dark, foggy days of the winter. The Marquis speaks lovingly about his camellias, naming each variety and discussing its characteristics. While we walk through the forest he is engulfed by vast box trees and his voice floats out of the trees as he talks of his family history and his own life story. He describes how as a young man he discovered the magic of camellias and how after a turbulent military career he rediscovered his adolescent passion. 'If only I hadn't forgotten them for so many years!'

LEFT: This bench is a reminder that the dense, damp and shady wood with its impressive old box trees has not always been here, but was planted in the seventeenth century. The Enlightenment thinker and politician Gaspar Melchor de Jovellanos wrote some of his most celebrated works seated here.

RIGHT: More than five hundred varieties of camellia grow here, including *Camellia japonica* 'Mathotiana', which covers the ground with a magic carpet of petals every winter.

ABOVE: There is an unmistakably Victorian flavour to this greenhouse, constructed at the end of the nineteenth century by Ivan Armada, one of the major contributors to the garden's development. Bromeliads and *Adiantum* grow in the pots.

RIGHT: Olive trees, rarely grown in northern Spain, form two intersecting avenues in the shape of a cross. This is the oldest part of the garden, planted in the sixteenth century when the medieval tower of Ortiguera was converted into a *pazo*. The silhouette of the owner among the trees highlights their striking size.

THE DOMÍNGUEZ FAMILY GARDEN

ALL FOR ONE AND ONE FOR ALL

In this area, gentle, humid coastal Galicia becomes more continental and austere. But it is still Galicia, still rainy, and with those familiar suave hills covered with pine trees and rounded outcrops of rock that look like whales in a sea of grass.

This garden has become a great communal living room shared by three families, all really one family: the family of Jesús Domínguez, who has his own textile business, the family of Adolfo Domínguez, the well-known fashion designer, and their mother, who instilled in her sons an enthusiasm for horticulture. It was she who devised the unusual mesh interlaced with wisteria which covers each house like a gift-wrapping.

The garden was designed by María Medina, who listened to everyone's ideas before beginning to shape the place. 'I immediately thought it was important to make use of the lovely stones scattered all around, and the water flowing so freely from the ground suggested to me that I should channel it into a specific place. So I united stones and water by making a lake. I played with the rocks – without moving any, we used them to outline the border of the lake. It brought life to the garden; the fish leapt in it and herons arrived. The austere landscape began to soften.'

Influenced by Adolfo and his taste for clean lines, María used poplars to trace straight avenues which invariably give on to clearings like open windows. Adolfo says, 'I love to look out at the silhouette of the poplars on misty days, and to hear the wind sighing in the leaves like the sound of the sea.'

The garden brings together the different natures of the Domínguez family. The rows of trees, the pond and the

sharp lines of the house satisfy Adolfo's rational sensibility and his taste for Japanese style, where everything is controlled and ordered despite the apparent simplicity and naturalness. Jesús, who is an enterprising and practical man, directed his considerable energies into helping the designer realize her scheme, finding solutions to problems as they occurred. Their mother's role was to fill the open spaces with life, adding flowers and other details – 'humanizing the design', as María Medina puts it.

María continues: 'I added dashes of colour and variety to the constant green of the pines surrounding the garden by planting deciduous trees like oak, birch and poplar, and clumps of camellias also add light and interest around the houses.' The icing on the cake was provided by an aunt who is a nun. A passionate gardener, she constructed a delightful kitchen garden, which is looked after and enjoyed by all.

'I want my gardens to be pleasing, for the mood to be right, for the owner to feel it is their own,' María says. She stresses the importance of light, of the play of sun and shade, and of the way a garden is brought to life by the changes it undergoes throughout the year.

It appears that she has achieved her end of pleasing the owners. 'When it was complete the family filed through the garden as though it was an enormous catwalk, the mother and the aunt both wearing Adolfo Domínguez outfits. The models suited the garden, and the garden suited the models.'

ABOVE: Rows of *Populus nigra* bring a sense of order and clarity very much in harmony with the ground cover of *Vinca minor*.

OPPOSITE: A cloud of multicoloured hydrangeas softens the strong lines of the house.

LEFT: *Wisteria sinensis* envelops the house. The space has the same simple elegance as the clothes of fashion designer Adolfo Domínguez, whose family share the garden. Beyond lie clumps of camellias.

RIGHT: The pond is an integral part of the garden's design. It appears to be natural but in fact the whole area had to be waterproofed in order to contain the water. The granite shape among the water lilies is like a whale surfacing at sea.

EL ABEO

OPPOSITE: The old vegetable patch has become an ornamental garden with flowers, fruit trees and aromatic plants. Lupins, kniphofias, centranthus and *Sedum spectabile* combine well in a colourful mass that is easily maintained. A 'Dorothy Perkins' rose climbs up the pear tree, which stands in front of an *horreo*, a traditional Asturian building used to protect grain from vermin and damp ground.

OVERLEAF: The orderly garden is surrounded by the lushness of nature. *Zantedeschia aethiopica* grows in the fountain and around it stand urns of *Pelargonium peltatum* next to spheres of *Buxus sempervirens*. Pots of hemerocallis are positioned by the railing.

BELOW LEFT: Moved stone by stone from its original location, the house is now covered by *Bougainvillea glabra*.

BELOW RIGHT: The rambling rose Cocktail decorates this arch, framing the surrounding landscape and linking it to the garden.

Nature, at its most abundant here, has paired spectacular mountains, caressed by the clouds that are ever present in the Asturias, with the musical echo of the stormy, misty sea. And where nature has been sculpting over the centuries man has not been idle.

The family who have owned this house since 1691 decided in 1968 to move it stone by stone to its current location close to Ribadasella, some kilometres away from the original site, where it was subsiding into a mine below the foundations. Moving it was an undertaking something like that of Americans who ship churches and palaces over from Europe in an attempt to buy time itself.

Once the house was set in its new position, between the sea and the mountains, it was necessary to create a garden around it. Several members of the family have been involved in this work. Isabel, the sister of the current owner, Jacobo Argüelles, designed a pool by the front door in the Hispano-Arabic style. Alongside it runs an arcade of trimmed cypresses that frame views of the sea. On the other side of the house Jacobo Argüelles and his wife, Alicia Pidal, have created a spacious raised meadow. This is splashed with bulbs and scattered with azaleas and rhododendrons, which serve to emphasize the mountains' colossal presence. At the centre of the meadow is a fountain and a hedged area.

The most recent addition comes from María Jesús Cagiga, the landscape designer of the family, who in 1996 created parterres on what had been a vegetable garden; these are bordered by lavender and box and hold a collection of old English roses, lupins and delphiniums.

Jacobo Argüelles is a banker, but these days he finds that his most precious asset is his garden. He confesses to finding more and more reasons to escape from Madrid and spend time here. 'In March I have to visit the sea of daffodils, in April I can't miss the azaleas and rhododendrons, in May it's the turn of the roses and then in July it's the hydrangeas . . .'

Carpe diem, as the saying goes.

ABOVE: Rhododendrons light up the garden in spring.

RIGHT: The patio to the front of the house is dominated by a long pool in the Hispano-Arabic style, full of water lilies and bordered by *Buxus sempervirens*. A cypress hedge with hollowed-out arches forms a living wall behind a bed of shrubby *Chamaecyparis,* plumbago and lantana.

COTUBÍN

THE ARCHITECTS' PENCIL

As happened so many times elsewhere, when I arrived in this garden its owners told me that it was not looking as good as it should this year. There had been no rain, so the garden did not have its usual lushness. But such is life; things are never perfect. When it rains we say it is sad; when the sun shines too much we call it a drought. And, as John Lennon put it, 'Life's what happens when you're busy making other plans.'

Plans, projects and experiments – that's what this garden, belonging to Spanish landscape gardener Luis González-Camino, is all about. It was from his father that he inherited the passion for gardens that he has had since he was a small boy. Luis explains: 'Whenever we went on a trip my father would test me and my sister on the names of all the trees and plants that we saw on the way. The tests became a game and made the journeys much more fun. When I was twelve or thirteen my father gave me a book about trees that confirmed my passion once and for all. The decisive moment came when, hoping to get me to focus my interest professionally, my mother suggested that I become a landscape gardener. From then on I studied and trained, and finally I became one.'

There is no need to ask Luis what gardening means to him. I have visited several of his gardens and seen for myself. Gardening defines him; he thinks it, feels it, loves it and works at it.

For Luis, light is all-important: 'You have to think about where the sun comes up at different times of the year. It's like a spotlight lighting up a stage. I am a photographer so I notice the sun, its light and intensity and the way it changes its angle with the seasons. All these things have an effect on the way we see the trees and plants of the garden. So throughout the garden we have to bear in mind the positioning of the plants, and the echoes and the contrasts that will be created.' All this and we haven't got on to the tricky subject of night-time lighting, about which there's so much to say, and still today so much to do in the search for nocturnal illumination that is both subtle and natural.

Luis continues, 'This is a team garden, the result of a dialogue between nature and us – that is to say, me, my brother Paco, who's an architect, and my French sister-in-law Françoise, who has added an Andalusian touch with the pots of colourful flowers.'

The lower part of the garden, where the house and lawns are, with its impressive trees, has a grand and romantic feel. It was started by Luis's great-grandfather, then continued by his grandfather and most recently by his father. In addition to planting several of the trees in this part of the garden Luis's father extended it upwards from the lower part by creating winding paths lined by azalea, beech, birch and oak.

In the place where his father created a single flowerbed with a pool in its centre, Luis has laid out a collection of colourful beds. 'This is my testing ground for other gardens. I experiment with plants I've bought abroad as well as with different ways of looking after them. In the old part of the garden we are letting the moss gradually invade the lawn; it gives it a magical, velvety texture. We use a blower to clean it so that it doesn't get damaged.' The garden is in a continuous state of expansion and evolution.

Luis shows his no-nonsense fondness for the garden in telling me about a sequoia which died after being struck by lightning. 'It was really hard saying goodbye to our giant friend who'd been with us for so long. Initially we thought of sculpting a totem pole but that would have cost a fortune so in the end we made something simpler: a pencil – maybe the largest pencil in the world.' Well, both the brothers are architects.

ABOVE: A wooden slatted window with the rose 'Zéphirine Drouhin'.

OPPOSITE: The *Sequoia sempervirens* trunk at the entrance to the garden is a surprising sight. The tree died when it was struck by lightning and it has since been wittily reincarnated as a giant pencil. Next to it sits a topiary cockerel. A rose bush and pots of *impatiens* add colour.

OVERLEAF LEFT: These beds, forming the centrepiece of the garden, are garden designer González-Camino's testing ground. The wide variety of plants he grows here includes Californian poppies, *Santolina chamaecyparissus*, *Erigeron karvinskianus*, *Achillea millefolium* and irises. At the centre is a pond with water plants.

OVERLEAF RIGHT: The typically Cantabrian simplicity of the green countryside and the house contrasts with the profusion of colour in the flowerbeds.

CENTRAL SPAIN

ÁBALOS

A ROOM WITH A VIEW

This garden basks in a place where the vines, aligned like an army on earthy carpets of brown, ochre and red, surrender to us the nectar that is Riojan wine, child of the union between the Cantabrian air and the Mediterranean sun.

The garden at Ábalos is like an elaborate tapestry laid at the feet of the house. It is arrayed to please the eye, to offer a view of nature dominated by man and to delight the spirit with the repetition and order of its geometric box hedges, which contrast with the rugged Sierra Cantabrica beyond.

The garden itself clearly reveals an Italian influence, as do the loggias opening on to the views. Returning from Italy in the seventeenth century, Antonio Ramírez de la Piscina decided to remodel the old house and create a garden after the style of the country he so admired. The current owner explains, 'This design became diluted with time, until at the start of the twentieth century my father, the Marquis of Legarda, found the original plans and decided to restore the garden. To achieve this, he transplanted several box plants that grew on the nearest mountain.'

Today his son has cleared from the parterres the mass of seasonal flowers that had been there for so long. Their removal has given more sharpness and strength to the original design, which now communicates the spirit of the epoch in which the garden was created, infusing the whole with a sense of time standing still.

RIGHT: The garden was created at the end of the seventeenth century and retains its classical design, which complements work carried out at the same time on the south elevation of the house, including loggias on three storeys. Box parterres, designed to be seen from above, create a magnificent living tapestry.

FAR RIGHT, ABOVE: A view of the garden from the upper loggia. *Cryptomeria japonica* stands in front of *Cedrus deodara*.

FAR RIGHT, BELOW: Pelargoniums brighten the sombre lines of box and sand.

SAN SEGUNDO

STONES AND ROSES

Ávila, city of saints and stones, is the highest city in Spain at 1,100 metres/3,000 feet above sea level. It is surrounded by the steppes and snow-capped mountains of Spain's central plateau. Within its austere walls, and beneath this harsh climate, it hides a treasure inspired by Andalusia and with a Castilian soul: the garden of San Segundo, a miracle of colour, fragrance and joy protected from the outside world by the longest city wall in Europe, like the walled fortress of the Alhambra in Andalusia.

The garden is a dream and with skill and patience you can bring it to fruition no matter where you are. The garden was entrusted by the Viscount of Güell in 1921 to the Sevillian painter and landscape gardener Javier de Winthuysen. He turned what were a few vegetable plots into a highly structured garden with strikingly differentiated areas, each with its own mood. Like his paintings, these were infused with his poetic sensibility.

The current proprietor is the Marquis of Pozoblanco, a writer, doctor and gardener. 'The garden is laid out in the shape of a cross with a diamond in the middle,' he says, pointing out the pool. 'It's a variation on the cloister garden, but with an Hispano-Arabic influence throughout, with pools, fountains and borders. We know that there were originally a lot of fruit trees, but they didn't last in this harsh climate.' Since inheriting the house and garden from a great-uncle some years ago, this young enthusiast has taken on the task of restoring the garden to Winthuysen's original design. To do this he had to convince his wife to live all the year round in Ávila, leaving their busy life in Madrid. As a doctor he could find work, and as a writer he could find the time previously denied him. It was a 'downshift' from the buzz of the capital, through which he exchanged the multinational company where he was working as a doctor for a local hospital, and his squash racquet for a hoe.

'San Segundo was my uncle Paco's summer house. That's why the garden is so huge compared to the house, which is the size of a garden shed – that's exactly what it was. He brought five stone bulls, which are a Celto-Iberian design from the second century BC. He also made a pergola next to the reservoir, which we now use as a swimming pool. I like these additions to Winthuysen's work, but generally I'm trying to get back to what he originally intended.'

Working on the garden has given the Marquis more time to appreciate all that is exquisite and fine about it, how one feels simply being in the space itself and what one brings to the space as an individual. 'In a Zen garden, the only living thing might be the moss underfoot.' But as well as space the garden sings with colours. Irises, lilac and roses bloom in succession until the last of the roses is buried by the first snowfall. Used sparingly here, their simplicity contrasts with the profusion of stony browns and greys and all the shades of green.

As we say our farewells, we remember what Winthuysen wrote about the garden: 'A majestic solemnity is wedded to the grace of the new flower. At the nuptial feast, the fountains and the birds sing – art and nature in harmony – and the plants nourish us with their breath. Beauty is sustained and renewed in the crescendo of nature's music.'

LEFT: This 3,000 square metre/3,588 square yd plot nestles in the north-eastern corner of Ávila's city wall, which is a constant reference point throughout the garden. An octagonal pool reflects the sky, with the effect that it shines like a diamond among the roses.

LEFT AND ABOVE: Stonework features throughout the garden.

RIGHT, ABOVE AND BELOW: The view over the garden. Each of the levels, linked by steps, has its own distinct character. Rose beds provide the only notes of colour in a garden designed around green hedges.

OVERLEAF: The design of the garden stands out in the snow.

BELOW: Beside the swimming pool – one of many water features – sits a pergola built during the 1930s using Renaissance columns.

LA MIRADA

TERZA NATURA

It was when I was looking at an aerial photo of a farm belonging to my family that I first noticed the valley. Even though I had seen it plenty of times from the ground the new perspective had me transfixed. I thought to myself, 'The views from that place must be spectacular.'

It was as if I had seen the light: I became obsessed with the place. Initially it was difficult even to get to the head of the valley. But I did, and I'll never forget the sheer exultation at seeing it before me, a huge furrow gouged out of the broad plain by some prehistoric river.

For a whole year I would bring friends and loved ones to the valley so that they could help me decide where to build the house – and also partly because as soon as they saw this place they loved me a little more; they loved me for my view. The Portuguese have a name for places with a bench for admiring the view: *enamoradoiros*, places for falling in love. I was looking for such a place for the house I was going to build. I asked all my friends which part they liked best and where they thought the view was most impressive. After taking a lot of soundings, I eventually settled on a particularly peaceful spot. Its location in the valley was the inspiration for the design of the house. I wanted the architecture to be timeless, in harmony with nature – with the ivy and oaks surrounding it. I had fallen head over heels in love with the place; I was enchanted. My girlfriend and I would spend hours just gazing at it, not wanting to change a thing. But then she and I broke up and my passions changed direction: I threw myself into something I had hardly considered before – making a garden. I wanted to make a new relationship between myself and nature, by creating an artificial nature, a universe in my image and likeness – as they said in the Renaissance, a *terza natura*.

The house was still at an early stage when I launched into the garden. I wanted to start from scratch, so I pulled up the trees. That was a mistake I have regretted ever since.

I am reminded of my stupidity year after year as I see just how long an oak tree takes to grow in Castille. As the soil was pure chalk, I decided to get rid of it. Hoping to enable trees to grow tall in the future and provide the shade that I wanted, I added some eight hundred lorryloads of topsoil. By that stage the garden was worse than a wanton mistress – it was threatening to ruin me financially. Work stopped and for several years it remained untouched – it was beautiful soil but there was nothing in it. A desert. That was until I had the idea of starting an adopt-a-tree scheme. There are nineteen in my family, counting all my half-siblings, and I asked everyone to become a godparent to a tree. They agreed and each year at Christmas they received a photo of their 'godchild'.

Now that the garden is starting to come together, I am pleased that I was able to put right my early mistakes. I have incorporated ilex and oaks from the indigenous woodland into the design of the garden. I have also used dead trees from the surrounding area as one of the basic and most characteristic elements of the garden, by converting them, with their bare branches, into dancing sculptures that contrast with and enliven the other trees. Other sculptures – mainly made from concrete – came from a need to fill the place with something happy and playful, giving the space a kind and generous feeling. In other words, I've treated my corner of the earth in the way I would like the earth to treat me.

ABOVE: Two sculpture-trees, terracotta-tinted, frame the central view of Eduardo Mencos' own garden.

OPPOSITE: Cement mixed with powdered iron runs between pools of glass and terracotta spheres. At the back is a pergola made of iron sheets with oval windows that diminish in size, exaggerating the perspective.

OVERLEAF: In the foreground, a hollowed-out bowl filled with ivy and cypresses is surrounded by gravel with serpentine forms in tinted cement. On the right, glass fragments salvaged from burgled cars cover the trunk of a dead holly oak.

LEFT: Concrete cones form a temple with a holly oak at the centre. Ampelopsis grows on the iron pergola beyond.

RIGHT: The organic shapes and earthy tones of the ivy-covered house provide a balance between architecture and nature. Here the house is reflected in an irregularly shaped pool containing water lilies and the author's sons, Gaspar and Pelayo.

EL MONASTERIO
BEAUTIFUL RUINS

Like a flower blooming on a wasteland, this is one of the jewels of recent Spanish garden design. A meeting of the past and present, it is the result of a collaboration between five people, each with their own contrasting ideas which have been combined to harmonious effect.

The old monastery in Castile was built in 1480. It was gutted by Napoleon's troops during the War of Independence and then, like many ecclesiastical properties at the time, it was auctioned off by the government. It had several owners before passing into the hands of the current owner's father in 1945.

It was 1985 before the family embarked on creating this serene, elegant and delightful garden, converting what were by now the ruins of the monastery into a splendid setting for their horticultural dreams.

To start with, the owners engaged Leandro Silva, the most renowned Spanish landscape gardener of the 1980s, who used olive trees from the surrounding property to create an avenue which leads up to the front door. Silva also proposed a long stairway down to a pool with a stone cross at the bottom. These designs were then realized by the architect Ignacio Vicens, who also designed and constructed the water maze.

'When we saw how the "creature" was taking such a pleasing shape, we got more involved and more passionate, and started to do things ourselves,' say the owners, as we cross the garden in July's heady warmth. 'Professor Vicens is an enthusiastic and brilliant architect. We consider him

part of the family, and he himself has adopted this place and added some wonderful touches of his own.'

Every visit to the garden brings fresh surprises, because there is always something new. Most recently the New Zealand gardener Christopher Masson has added a secluded little retreat.

As in so many places in Spain where three cultures flourished during the Middle Ages – Christian, Jewish and Arab – here we find a fruitful mixture of people and ideas. There is an emphasis on the Hispano-Arabic tradition with its stairways, pools and narrow canals. In other parts there are simple elegant cloisters made out of laurel, grass and ivy, which marry so well with the stone ruins. And we move from the straight and clear lines of the laurel maze to the symbolic slenderness of the water maze, walled by cypresses, which invites us to the spiritual search, making us see the metaphorical meaning of the maze as an expression of the human journey through life. The common 'argument' that one can see and hear throughout the garden is water; the repetitive and musical murmur of nature's prayers, guided by man.

ABOVE: Ivy and laurel furnish this tranquil garden in the ruined cloister of a fifteenth-century Augustinian monastery. White roses recall the monks' veneration of the Virgin.

RIGHT: The garden stretches down from the west side of the house in a series of green 'rooms'. Its backbone is a flight of Hispano-Arabic-style steps over which narrow channels of water flow down to the rectangular pool below. The steps are flanked by rows of *Cupressus sempervirens* 'Stricta'.

RIGHT ABOVE: Thirty-two ancient olive trees create a shady and majestic welcome to the garden.

RIGHT BELOW: At the foot of the series of waterfalls is this long, narrow pool with white water lilies and spheres of box sitting alongside.

OPPOSITE ABOVE: The water maze enclosed within walls of cypress is resonant with symbolism.

OPPOSITE BELOW: The architectural lines and fresh green of a laurel maze stand out against the brick and stone of the monastery.

OVERLEAF: Between the water steps and the mazes lies this sea of *Agapanthus africanus* and *A.* 'Alice Gloucester'. They combine beautifully with the lushness of a tamarix and the solid vertical lines of cypresses.

PALACIO DE GALIANA

A PERFECT MARRIAGE

This garden in Toledo looks as if it has partnered the ancient Palacio de Galiana for centuries, but it is only some forty years old. The elegance and simplicity of the place has been captured through the sensibility and wisdom of its creator, Carmen Marañón.

The bulk of the construction was built in the hybrid Christian-Arab Mudéjar style by Alfonso X 'the Wise' in the thirteenth century, on the site of an earlier Moorish palace known as the Pavilion of the Water Wheel. The legend goes that the Taifa king al-Ma'mun would retire to its glass dome to listen to the waters. These were drawn from the nearby river by a water wheel, whose foundations are still visible. Contemporary reports describe the palace as one of the most beautiful in the world, lying amid gardens and orchards, containing hundreds of species that made it the first botanical garden in Europe.

Following centuries of neglect, the palace was a ruin when the current owner, Carmen Marañón, daughter of the doctor and intellectual Gregorio Marañón, bought it in the late 1950s with her husband Alejandro Fernández-Araoz. After a thorough survey and lengthy consultation with architects Manuel Gómez Moreno and Fernando Chueca Goitia, they began a sensitive restoration of the building. To avoid having to make any changes to the original structure, they decided not to live in the palace and to build a completely new home near by in a traditional Toledan style.

Sofía Barroso, Carmen's granddaughter, explains, 'Restoring Galiana in the 1960s was my grandmother's way of getting over the death of her beloved father. When her husband died shortly afterwards, she threw all her energy and passion into creating a garden from scratch. This served as a pressure valve and was a source of great satisfaction.' Discussing the influences on the garden's design, she mentions her grandmother's visits to the Alhambra and the Generalife. 'An important inspiration, Eduardo, was the conversations my grandmother had with your grandmother [the Marquesa de Casa Valdés]. My grandmother frequently referred to the Marquesa's book *Gardens of Spain* and it helped to clarify her ideas.'

Used as a sculptural element, cypress dominates the garden. Its rigorous pruning lends the place a strikingly ascetic and elegant air. Or, as Carmen used to say, 'With their trunks wrapped in ivy, the cypresses look as if they're floating, suspended in space, and this gives them a metaphysical quality. They're like a geyser of dreams, or a passionate prayer cast up to the sky.'

FAR LEFT: Slender columns and filigreed arches – a splendid example of fourteenth-century Mudéjar style – frame a view of the foundations of King Taifa al-Ma'mun's eleventh-century water wheel.

LEFT: A view of the palace from the old vegetable garden on the banks of the River Tajo. Bricks form a herringbone pattern on the central path, which is bordered by privet and philadelphus.

RIGHT: Two elegant cypresses appear to watch over Toledo's iconic skyline in the distance.

OVERLEAF: The patio, seen from one of the palace towers. Water, cypress and ivy are used as architectural elements.

LAS NAVAS

HUNTING BEAUTY

Where once it smelt of gunpowder, today it smells of flowers. The Las Navas estate in the hills near Toledo looks on to a wild and limitless landscape where deer, boar and other game roam free. As with many such estates in recent years, there has been an attempt to provide a human counterpoint to the untamed surroundings. In this case a beautiful balance has been achieved.

It feels more like Kenya than Europe here: the uninhabited spaces, the light, and the sounds of the wild animals recall Karen Blixen's novel *Out of Africa*. However, the garden is profoundly Mediterranean, elegant and fully aware of its incredible location. As normally happens in Spain, the women of the house started things off in the garden. In 1988 they invited the landscape gardener Leandro Silva to work with them. The pergola over the swimming pool, the abundant lavender, the greenhouse and four cypresses on the patio date from this period. However, things did not run smoothly and, since they had grand ambitions and a generous budget, they decided to aim higher and engaged the Anglo-Italian designer Arabella Lennox-Boyd.

'She came to have a look at the desolate landscape one February, in the middle of a severe frost, and pronounced that nothing would grow here,' the proprietor explains. 'Afterwards we went to the Botanical Gardens in Madrid and she asked me what I wanted. Playing devil's advocate, I reminded her of how harsh our climate is, our "nine months of winter and three months of hell" – referring to our very hot summers. In fact we were both discouraging each other.' Lengthy discussions ensued and despite her

reservations she agreed to do a design. 'Arabella was relentless in her questioning, talking about the project as though it were a child. You hand over your garden to someone and it's as if you've bought a puppy from them – you know they'll be back in a year to check up on it. So we tried to find some common ground. The key was uncovering the landscape, which had been obscured by different plants. We wanted the garden to have openings – windows on to the plain and its seasonal changes.' At the same time they wanted an Hispano-Arabic feel. This normally means a degree of enclosure, but they arrived at a fusion of English and Hispanic styles with some Italian touches.

Arabella Lennox-Boyd proposed two alternative designs, one with water and one without. 'We went for water, and enthusiastically got on with the project ourselves. We shifted a lot of soil and brought in trees and plants from England, France, Italy and Spain.'

The cypresses work as a crucial architectural element, helping to compartmentalize the space and highlighting the sense of perspective in the striking vistas. 'We decided on the column shapes ourselves. Our gardener handles a sickle extremely well, shaving them into sculptures that bring sharpness and order.

'Two years passed between Arabella's first visit and her return to see the design she'd left with so much scepticism. During this time we had worked, learned, planted, suffered and enjoyed ourselves. When she saw what we had done she was fascinated and admired how handsomely we had carried through her – our – creation. The hard work was worth it.'

OPPOSITE: A 'crown' of cypresses emphasizes the entrance to the house and garden. 'Out Yonder' irises and 'Zéphirine Drouhin' roses grow in the foreground.

ABOVE: The cypresses form freestanding columns, complementing the wide horizons beyond. In the foreground *Phlomis fruticosa* and white centranthus bloom.

BELOW TOP: An iron pergola, covered in 'Guinée' and 'Madame Grégoire Staechelin' roses, emerges from four broad box hedges.

BELOW BOTTOM: A pergola covered in White Bells roses offers a place to enjoy the view. Lavender grows in the foreground.

RIGHT: A statue of Triton blows water from a seashell in the middle of this cross-shaped pond full of callas and water lilies. *Salvia lavandulifolia* grows around box parterres, which hold sculpted Iceberg rose bushes.

ABOVE: This level area functions as an enormous viewing platform looking out to the soft curves of the nearby hills. The play of greens and the simple shapes form a whole that is divided into 'rooms' by hedges of box and cypress. A secluded central space has been created for a pool.

OPPOSITE: Lavender and 'Out Yonder' irises grow around the cypresses and a welcoming fountain at the main entrance to the house.

BELOW: Inspired by a drawing of the Villa Lante in Italy, this smooth cascade runs between spheres of *Buxus sempervirens* 'Rotundifolia'. The paths on either side are made of pebbles set in cement.

PALACIO CHAVES MENDOZA

DECORATING WITH NATURE

Trujillo is steeped in Spanish history, with its universal symbols: churches, castles and conquistadores. Here the conquistador Francisco Pizarro herded swine as he imagined the gold of the Americas.

For some years now, the interior designer Duarte Pinto-Coelho has had a house here in a converted convent which looks out over the stark and infinite plains of Extremadura to his native Portugal. He has created a garden in his own style: baroque, classical and eclectic. Though I had not met Duarte before, as I entered the garden I immediately felt as though I knew him, which made me think of the Spanish philosopher María Zambrano's phrase, 'a garden is the architecture of the soul'.

Duarte extended his style from the house into the garden, despite the intense summer, the scarcity of water and the bitter cold of winter. 'Making these rooms without roofs I was forcibly reminded of nature, and of where I was.' It truly is a garden of rooms – patios and terraces which have grown ever more complicated as their creator amuses himself.

'A country house without a garden is like a body without a soul. The house is static but the garden grows, whether you like it or not. It always surprises you, it's alive. This garden gives you everything – its fruits, artichokes, lemons, tomatoes. It's an enormous pleasure to eat them whilst you walk in this beautiful place. They are the legacy of the kitchen garden maintained for centuries by the Carmelite nuns who were here before me. It also gives me flowers, and depending on the season I flood the house with cut hydrangeas, roses and arum lilies.'

The weather affects Duarte more now that he has a garden. He pays for droughts, he confesses, with vast water bills, while rain brings thoughts of the future and peace.

'Being an interior designer has helped me with the garden, but so have my travels, and encouragement from my gardener friends who help me and compliment me on the garden. It's certainly made a difference that I grew up in Cascais in Portugal, where everyone has a garden and they compete to see who has the best dahlias or hydrangeas. In Portugal we've been very influenced by the English, who have passed on their skills and love of gardening. For me a garden has to be welcoming; it invites you to be yourself, to feel at ease, to stay a while. Sometimes looking at modern gardens I think they're only made to look good in photos.'

He reflects on what gardening has given him. 'Two years ago I popped out into the garden one day and it was just dazzling, overwhelming: I counted seventy varieties of flowers. What an explosion, what a marvel, what pleasure! And I can't forget the other great lesson I've learned – respect for nature and her "*tempo*". I tend to want everything done yesterday, but I've learnt in the garden not to be impatient. The wait is a pleasure too.'

OPPOSITE, ABOVE LEFT: The kitchen garden, which contains aromatic and medicinal plants, is an integral part of the garden. Santolina borders the walkway; artichokes are in the foreground.

OPPOSITE, ABOVE RIGHT: Classical sculptures – which the designer also uses in interiors – enliven various corners of the garden. 'Elvinhall' irises bloom here in May.

OPPOSITE, BELOW: Topiary in simple playful shapes contrasts with the formal lines of nearby buildings and the colourful *Prunus pissardii* in the foreground.

BELOW: *Nepeta* 'Six Hills Giant' and *Stachys byzantina* surround a bust of Ceres, goddess of abundance.

LA ROMERA

La Mancha, that region of wine and wheat, means 'dry land' in Arabic. The adventures of Don Quixote are set amid this cruel terrain, which still presents a challenge for any gardener today. Like Don Quixote, the owners of La Romera have not flinched before their enemy – the rugged climate with its harsh winters and torrid summers – and they have cultivated plants such as azaleas and rhododendrons previously unheard of in this area. In fact La Romera is living proof that a garden is a wish and that given the will and the wherewithal it can come true anywhere.

Starting with a modest lodge, the owners extended the living space and created a series of patios to the rear, all different but all featuring water and flowers. Each of the bedrooms looks on to a patio – that great Roman invention gracefully developed by the Moors. The design is inspired by the Hispano-Arabic style. With its mingling of cultures, this style is still a source of inspiration for many new gardens, which continue to have an unparalleled feeling of freshness, safety and peace.

The front garden was set out by the landscape gardener Ricardo Villalta, and includes a water spiral on the ground that 'swallows' the water of the swimming pool, a parterre of box and catalpa, paved areas and borders. 'The more the garden grew, the more my husband loved it,' says the owner. 'He went from being a client to designing some areas himself, and his enthusiasm was infectious. We adored the Alhambra, and we wanted this place to ooze the same essence with patios, streams and fountains.'

The owner was widowed several years ago and has found solace in her garden. 'It's one of the most inspiring things in life, an immense comfort. It heightens my awareness of the changing seasons, and the differences between one year and the next. It teaches me to look forward to the blooming of every flower or to try planting something which wasn't there before.

'My husband would come back from the office and stroll through the garden, and if he saw that something wasn't working then he changed it. He enjoyed taking decisions, and a garden is a constant flow of choices.' Now she and her son are inspired by a new project: another impossible garden in a difficult place, this time a castle in Spain's coldest region. Life does go on.

RIGHT: The use of water here is fully in keeping with Hispano-Arabic tradition. The water flows from the upper pool over an iron sheet, slips down a narrow channel, runs into a swimming pool and finally sinks into a spiral.

BELOW: Balls of box, protected from the elements by *Catalpa bungei*, contrast with the texture of the stones. *Lonicera nitida* cascades over the low wall on the left.

LEFT: At the centre of this patio, water springs from a font that seems to float above a carpet of ground-cover roses. Iron in the water has given the stones a reddish tone.

RIGHT AND BELOW TOP: Three patios with fountains – water takes centre stage in this garden. The pots contain *Pelargonium zonale*.

BELOW BOTTOM: A view of the house from the upper pool of the water feature on the previous page. Close to the house are specimens of *Magnolia grandiflora*.

THE SOUTH

CARMEN DE LA JUSTICIA

THE MUSIC OF THE SENSES

Back in the eighteenth century, the administration of the Alhambra palace in Granada found itself lacking money and unable to pay the bills of two of its gardeners. Needing to somehow honour the debt, the administration signed over to them a plot of land next to one of the palace entrances – the Gate of Justice – by way of payment.

The artist behind this garden is the present owner, a sprightly ninety-four-year-old lady who, like all good gardeners, considers her work of art to be unfinished, making changes and adding new ideas every day as if the garden is letting her forget her mortality. María tells me, 'I was born in Granada and spent all my childhood here. When I started this garden in 1939 I already knew the Alhambra and the Generalife palaces like the back of my hand. In those days people used not to visit the Alhambra; there were many influential people from Granada who had reached the age of fifty or more without ever setting foot inside. But I thought it was glorious. My brothers and I used to ride our horses around the gardens. We grew up there; that's where we learned to see what is good and what is bad.' After the Civil War, when life in Spain was bleak, María turned to this garden and the life flourishing there to find hope for her future.

The terraces and many of the older trees – the cypresses, palms and wisteria – were already in place when María started on the garden, as were many of the fruit trees. 'I decided to bring structure to what was already there. First of all I enlarged the reservoir into a swimming pool and made it look much nicer. Then I planted box in circle and star shapes to smarten up the main terrace. I wanted each one to contain only one type of flower, but my gardener, Manuel, kept managing to mix up the plants and what resulted was a potpourri of colours. After a number of

other mix-ups I came across him one day busily pulling out some beautiful red roses. I could have killed him, but he just turned to me and solemnly asked, "Why would you want to keep these, *señora*? The leaves and the flowers look just the same." That explained everything – Manuel was colour blind.'

Manuel remained dedicated to the garden until his retirement and even afterwards he would come to see it every day, like a faithful lover. 'One day I noticed that various tools kept appearing in our garden: ladders, shears, mattocks. I said to him, "But Manuel, you have always been good and loyal. How come you are taking things from the Alhambra? You will go to hell for stealing." And he simply replied, 'No, *señora*, they're not for me, they're for the garden.'

María frets about the garden's future and the guardian angel it will need. 'I now have a grandson, Alfonso, which encourages me and makes me want to see that the garden keeps improving.' She continues, 'I think about how grateful nature is. You can give everything to a person and still they let you down, but if you give your garden patience, work, money and care it will respond. I believe that plants answer if you speak to them. I remember going up to a magnolia one very hot day in the Generalife to pick a flower. I opened it up, smelt it and stroked my cheek with one of its petals. It was such an intoxicating feeling, with its perfume and its subtle voluptuous sensuality. In those surroundings, with the sound and sight of water, I realized that a garden refines and condenses things into a kind of music of the senses.'

ABOVE: A view of the Alhambra with the Sierra Nevada range beyond.

LEFT: A pergola clad in *Wisteria sinensis* with irises at its feet forms an enchanting tunnel.

FAR LEFT: The garden's terraced design is clearly visible from the pool.

CENTRE LEFT: A path lined by *Paeonia suffruticosa*.

LEFT: The ancient tower of the Alhambra's Gate of Justice forms part of the garden.

BELOW LEFT: *Lagerstroemia indica* grows from a box parterre, which also holds dahlias, *Phlox paniculata* and hollyhocks (*Alcea rosea*).

BELOW CENTRE: The view from the villa. In the foreground is *Wisteria sinensis* and beyond that a red *Cercis siliquastrum*.

BELOW RIGHT: The lower terrace, with shapes in box and a bed of *Lavandula angustifolia*.

MORATALLA

THE REVITALIZER

ABOVE: A sunken patio with a circular pool.

RIGHT: Through the centuries the spiral has been a potent symbol of unity and infinity for many cultures. This feature combines water and brick.

OPPOSITE: This majestic garden is something of a hybrid in the 'neo-Sevillian' style of Forestier, who started work on it in 1915. It combines the sweeping vistas of the French idiom with details straight from the Hispano-Arabic tradition – low fountains, tiles and brickwork. Cypresses (*Cupressus sempervirens* and *C. arizonica*), oleanders and mimosas add perspective.

OVERLEAF: Beside the house an immense vault formed by the branches of plane trees creates a cool, damp microclimate, out of the searing heat of the region. A sea of *Agapanthus africanus* gives a bluish light in the shade of the trees.

The Duke of Segorbe, owner of this garden, is the co-proprietor of some of the most important gardens in Spain such as Pazo de Oca in Galicia and Palacio de Pilatos in Seville, which belong to one of Spain's oldest noble families, the Medicaneli. He has taken on the restoration and improvement of these gardens with exemplary determination and energy.

'I don't enjoy gardens passively,' the Duke says. 'What I like to do is shape them, to look in the archives to find out how they were and to return them to their former splendour. I'm restless and I need something to happen in them. I'm planning a new landscape garden here,' he points out as we pass a stream bordered by arum lilies.

The Duke was greatly influenced by his tutor Santiago Amon, who was interested in garden design and who considered a garden to be a form of 'living architecture'. 'Movement is important, because you have to be aware of more than the present when you make a garden: you have to predict the future. Conceptually, I'm very interested in the gardens of classical mythology, the Hesperides, Eden . . .' Other important influences were Russell Page and Salvador Dalí, a great friend who shared the Duke's keen interest in mythology.

But aside from the philosophy the Duke is a practical man: 'In recent years we have reached a point where the gardens at Oca and Pilatos are self-supporting. They make enough from admission charges to be well maintained and for us to be able to continue with improvements. I hope that Moratalla will soon be in the same position.'

Moratalla is Arabic for 'the Moor's lookout', named after a fortress from the Middle Ages. A number of Roman villas in the area suggest that before that it was a holiday spot for local landowners here in 'Rome's breadbasket'.

Looking at a majestic span of plane trees, and talking about the history of the garden and the contribution of Forestier, the great French landscape gardener who had so much influence in Spain in the early twentieth century, the Duke explains, 'These trees were not planted by Forestier. Moratalla was a romantic English garden in the nineteenth century

and it gradually became more formal. It could be that the effect of the span was created more by chance than design. In fact, chance is the most important thing in this garden.' However, Forestier did contribute a great cypress avenue with fourteen patios. Their design is a characteristically neo-Arabic assembly of ceramics, tiles, streams and low fountains. 'Forestier was a Frenchman who immersed himself in Spain, who found our past for us,' the Duke comments. 'But when I see the grand avenue with that gate at the end, I can't help but think that with that central axis and that perspective he never quite stopped being French.'

FAR LEFT: Steps alongside the great avenue lead down to a shady area. The columns soak up the last rays of the sun. The urns contain *Nephrolepis* ferns.

LEFT ABOVE: Trailing geraniums and a Portuguese-style gazebo.

LEFT BELOW: Not only does this arbour on the patio at the entrance to the house give welcome shade, but the *Rosa banksiae* create a magical tapestry of colour, light and shadow.

PALACIO DE LAS DUEÑAS

THE REALM OF THE SENSES

'My childhood is the memory of a lemon tree on a Sevillian patio,' begins one of Antonio Machado's most beautiful poems. The great poet was born in one of the houses found by the patios of the Palacio de las Dueñas, belonging to the Dukes of Alba.

This is a garden that is a series of gardens, opening out like a crown, with the main courtyard of the palace at its centre. Here is a space full of the sensual and exotic, dominated by a tiled fountain and surrounded by an arched Renaissance-style gallery.

'This courtyard has always been like the palace's great salon, where the important events take place,' explains the Duchess of Alba, a keen gardener. (As well as being a grand Spanish aristocrat and owner of more titles than anyone, she is one of the very few people not obliged by protocol to bow before the Queen of England.)

The Palacio de las Dueñas, in the centre of Seville, was begun in the fourteenth century and the main part completed in the fifteenth century. Since then it is the garden that has changed, with additions through the years up to the innovations of the current Duchess.

Beneath the trilling of a thousand birds Duchess Cayetana speaks enthusiastically about the garden to which she is devoted. 'I didn't want a very set garden – I wanted a joyful space with a great mixture of flowers.'

This unaffected taste is characteristic of Seville's aristocratic homes, and is evidenced by the pool, where pots full of flowers in blazing colours are suggestive of a humble neighbourhood patio. The Palacio de las Dueñas is an unorthodox place, home to kings and poets born of different cultures, anchored by its history but at the same time open to the future. The Duchess says that whenever a neighbouring property falls vacant she demolishes it to make way for a new garden filled with colour and perfume to ravish the senses.

ABOVE: An urn containing pelargoniums bears the crest of the palace.

OPPOSITE: The central patio is the nucleus of this garden. It is surrounded by galleries of Renaissance design decorated by Mudéjar plasterwork. Low euonymus hedges define colourful beds of roses, geraniums and daisies, converging on a tiled fountain planted with a mass of calla lilies.

ABOVE LEFT: One of the palace's seven patios.

ABOVE RIGHT: A high marble fountain among roses.

RIGHT: A water tank with pots of *Chlorophytum elatum* and an enormous fig tree. The tank serves as a reservoir and a pool, and its water makes a mirror reflecting the space.

BELOW LEFT: The Duchess of Alba in front of a tapestry of *Bougainvillea glabra*.

BELOW RIGHT: A *Cycas revoluta* among the arches.

OPPOSITE: This cross-shaped garden formed by box hedges runs on from the main patio. In the centre is a low octagonal fountain, decorated with tiles in the Hispano-Arabic manner.

CORTIJO DE LOPA

FROM PIGS TO FLOWERS

Many of the gardens in this book belong to palaces, monasteries and other noble houses loaded with history and brimming with their own stories, where famous gardeners have worked to augment the grandeur of the buildings. In contrast the garden at Lopa is all about bare simplicity and harmony with the Andalusian countryside. In what is inevitably a subjective evaluation of a garden's quality, this restraint and elegance was what caught my eye and seduced me. Here is a garden where I felt at ease, and where I enjoyed the charm of its creator, the owner Concha Ybarra.

With wisdom and a sure hand, Concha has found the spirit of this old place, where olive trees bring order to the landscape and the farm buildings form an oasis of life, both human and animal. Her touch is most evident in the garden, whose burgeoning development has not been at the expense of the past.

'The patio is one of the key features of Andalusian architecture, both in the town and the country,' she explains. 'In Lopa it serves the needs of a working estate.' The front patio is a mounting step, where horses are watered and prepared. It is by the stables and the homes of the estate workers, who gather here at dusk to enjoy the freshness of the orange trees, and the scent of jasmines and honeysuckle.

It is the other patio, reached through the house, that contains the intimate family garden. This is all Concha's own work. She banished the pigs that used to live here and planted flowers and trees in their place: bougainvilleas, roses, fig trees, palms, immense cacti and an infinity of flowerpots. This floral universe is animated by ducks, geese, hens, rabbits, turkeys, doves and other animals which pass freely through the garden.

Every May, 'the month of the Virgin', thousands of pilgrims from all over Spain make the journey to the famous shrine at nearby Rocío, many of them passing through Lopa to hear mass in the estate chapel. Concha, the mistress of ceremonies, talks excitedly of the big day, explaining how the patio receives the 'Rocieros' with a smile of welcome. 'It's pure spectacle: the men wear traditional costume and the women dress up in flamenco dresses, which blend with the shapes and colours of the flowers.'

ABOVE LEFT: Every May, pilgrims on their way to the nearby shrine at Rocío stop here to rest and pray.

ABOVE RIGHT: Hens are also a part of the garden.

LEFT: Bougainvillea and daisies make the entrance to the chapel an explosion of colour.

OPPOSITE: Two orange trees preside over the entrance to the house. Pots of pelargoniums on the wall, brightly tiled benches and *albero* – an ochre-coloured sand – give a genuine flavour of Andalusia.

ABOVE: The drinking trough for horses is at the centre of the front patio. Mallows grow at the feet of the orange trees.

BELOW: Palms create a colonnade along this path lined with *Canna indica*.

RIGHT: Whitewashed bricks define the edge of this mixed border. *Yucca gloriosa*, tall euphorbias and different types of palm trees including *Phoenix dactylifera* create the permanent structure of the garden. In the foreground are hollyhocks (*Alcea rosea*) and larkspur (*Consolida*).

EL BOTÁNICO,
SANLÚCAR DE BARRAMEDA

YOUNG AT HEART

Reaching up to the sky and dancing in the wind like giant tufty ears of corn, the palm trees welcome me. Standing to attention like a wall of soldiers they are both the guardians and the stars of El Botánico in Sanlúcar de Barrameda.

The garden got its name at the beginning of the nineteenth century, when it started life as an acclimatization zone for plants brought from the Americas. The idea came from the then prime minister Godoy, but during the uprisings of 1808 the people of Sanlúcar razed it to the ground, leaving nothing here but the name.

In the mid-nineteenth century the estate was bought for its plentiful water supply and fertile ground by Don Antonio de Orleans, who was heir to the French throne and married to the sister of Isabel II of Spain. Sanlúcar de Barrameda could be easily reached from Seville via the Guadalquivir River. Its mild climate and fabulous sunsets enchanted Don Antonio, who used to spend his summers

here. Together his descendants and the land have seen many changes. One character who particularly stands out is Don Ataúlfo. It was he who planted the tufty palms or 'palms in their nightgowns', as he called them.

His sister-in-law Carla de Orleans has been the latest to bring new life and innovations to this garden. Now aged eighty-seven, she says the garden gave her strength, light and hope when she was widowed shortly after moving here. It is not the first time that a garden has consoled the troubled or offered comfort to the lonely, but this is a special case. Where once the only plants were the palms and the Jupiter trees (*Lagerstroemia indica*), a frail widow in poor health has created a flourishing garden almost from scratch. Carla explains, 'I decided that the garden ought to be Andalusian, full of flowers, colour and greenery; there should be nothing sophisticated about it, it should not require much attention and it should always be lush

whenever I came here. So I planted plenty of perennials and lilies, as well as a great deal of bougainvillea, which always flowers so much. I sketched out paths – little walkways that wind through the garden and allow me to move about, to touch and to smell nature.' Neither did she forget about the seasons. 'I want the sun to touch me, to be able to feel it on my skin. At the same time, I don't want the paths to become a quagmire. So I'm putting in a lot of deciduous trees, like the grove of fig trees which I'm having planted at the moment. Every shady spot has its own smell and feel, and a distinctive texture. It's important to bear these subtleties in mind. The oak doesn't give the same type of shade as the fig tree.'

Her daughter, Beatriz, joins us. 'Every morning when my mother wakes up she immediately takes the lift down from her bedroom in the tower to the garden. She loves it so much – she tours through the pathways in her wheelchair like a young girl.' Carla continues, 'I still want to learn, and a garden teaches you so much: to find the best place for each tree; to move it when it isn't happy; to appreciate the light; to look for the shade. You learn that every part has its own content, and that there is always a place to sit and to be, just be . . . The palms are marvellous filters for the light. They make it dance so beautifully – it's quite a sight. Once when I was in Rome my brother-in-law Ataúlfo called me up, terrified, saying, "Carla, something ghastly has happened! A nightshirt on one of the palms has fallen off!" To cheer him up I rather cheekily said, "Well now, Ataúlfo, just you wait and see how gorgeous they look when they are all naked!"'

BELOW LEFT: Palm trees (*Phoenix dactylifera*) grow in front of the main house. In the centre of the garden, *Bougainvillea glabra* flourishes around a well and *Amaryllis belladonna* encircles the pool.

BELOW RIGHT: An elegant flagstone path between oleanders.

ABOVE LEFT: A bandstand, clad in multicoloured bougainvillea and *Lantana camara*.

ABOVE RIGHT: The bare trunks of the palm trees support graceful bougainvillea.

LEFT: Two rows of *Lagerstroemia indica* add straight lines to a garden full of curves, and in the summer an explosion of colour.

OPPOSITE: Tall palm trees (*Washingtonia filifera*) grow by a winding path bordered with lilies and roses.

ALCUZCUZ

CROSSBREEDING

Perched on a sizeable hill looking out over the Mediterranean are the house and garden of interior designer Jaime Parladé and his wife, Janetta. Both the hill and the house are called Alcuzcuz and have belonged to the family for more than a hundred and fifty years. During that time they have suffered and survived the vicissitudes of the Costa del Sol, from fires and excessive tree felling to the devouring urban sprawl of today's Marbella.

'There are plenty of trees here that are over a hundred years old: palms, pines, rubber trees, orange, lemon, olive and carob trees. But over the years we've also introduced plants, including a very special collection of mimosas, some cypresses, and countless shrubs and perennials,' says Parladé. 'My attitude to the plants has changed a lot. These days I'm finding myself drawn to the greenness and the shapes of leaves and less interested in flowers, although I still can't stand reddish or variegated leaves.'

Here, and indeed along the whole Costa del Sol, the English landscape gardener Gerald Huggan has had a pronounced influence on the garden design and on the introduction of exotic species, particularly from Kenya.

Parladé explains how the first seeds of his love for plants and gardens were sown: 'I spent my childhood and adolescence in Tangiers where I would go out with my mother to the souk to buy exquisite flowers from the Riff women under the great ombu trees. I was deeply impressed by the gardens of our friends in the famous Vielle Montagne district of the city. Mostly our friends were English people who had retired from the colonies and the gardens were full of surprises and eccentricities. Plants were placed where they would grow best, not just where they would have most visual impact.' In the same city he made friends with Jamie Caffery, a great botanist and a magnificent gardener, who was the first person to create gardens on the Costa del Sol in the 1950s. He introduced many varieties of dates, *Jasminum polyanthum* and *Rosa* 'Mermaid'. 'I used to help him plant his gardens and he was a great mentor to me.'

With all this background it is no surprise that the garden at Alcuzcuz is an inexhaustible source of pleasure. 'I am

deeply involved with my garden and I find it hard to be away from it for more than a month.' Parladé loves to discuss changes in the layout, the species or pruning with his wife, or with anyone who will listen. 'I hope I haven't turned into what the English call a "garden bore",' he laughs.

ABOVE: This brick path winds through the shadiest part of the garden, flanked by aralias, *Hydrangea quercifolia* and *H. arborescens* 'Annabelle'. As a focal point, an iron statue stands above two inviting seats.

OPPOSITE: The warm climate means that this patio is usable all year round, as an extra room to the house. The ground is set with smooth pebbles; the pots contain box and *Senecio maritimus*.

OVERLEAF: This terraced garden is a blend of different influences. This corner alone contains a border, an English-style lawn, Mediterranean cypresses and a palm tree, which is evidence of the almost tropical climate.

ABOVE: An *Asparagus plumosus* springs from the mouth of the old well at the centre of this bed. To one side is a wild old rose bush. Cineraria and santolina make a pretty contrast with the box hedge.

OPPOSITE: Hills classically covered in Mediterranean pines and cypresses, seen from one of the terraces. Potted pelargoniums add colour in the foreground.

LEFT: With a decorator's eye, the owner has painted the walls of this chapel in light-hearted pink and white stripes and complemented them with brightly coloured bougainvillea.

LA ROZALEJA

A MEETING OF CULTURES

With a view of Africa but with the Mediterranean at its feet, La Rozaleja looks out from a smooth hill whose curves are brought to life by cork trees, Iberian in their warmth and exuberance, and their swaying figures sculptures of time and wind. The wind is an important character here, in the form of either the Atlantic bluster from the south-west or the heavy, damp easterly levanter from over the Mediterranean. The garden breathes best when the wind is in the east.

La Rozaleja, close to Gibraltar, has reached its current splendid state over the last few years, coinciding with the maturing of its owners and the benign impact of the New Zealand landscape gardener Christopher Masson. He describes it thus: 'Both the elevation of the plot and the varying types of terrain make this garden stand out from other gardens in built-up areas. Russell Page sculpted the land and from the beginning the idea was to achieve a sense of space, of losing oneself, by doing away with the boundaries. That was his genius.' As we pass along an emerald green tongue of lawn which leads to a wooden cabin looking out over the sea, Christopher explains that when he arrived, although the main elements of the garden were already in place, they needed to be brought into sharper focus. 'The broad sweeps Russell Page had proposed were there but what had been lost over the years was any definition in borders or planting. Some of the shrubs were blending into each other and there was a lack of textural excitement from contrasting foliage.'

Asked to consider the difficulties the garden has presented, he immediately mentions the problem of drainage. 'Sometimes excessive irrigation systems in this part of the world cause problems, so it is vital to have an efficient means of allowing water to run off. Plants which have adapted for hot climates thrive in well-drained soil and they can put up with drought conditions but are so often killed with kindness. We have overcome many of these problems. I maintain that building up the soil above the general level of the land ensures good drainage.'

Our conversation moves to that crucial element for a landscape gardener, his relationship with the owners. In this case the meeting seems to have been a happy one for all. The Spanish-Filipino owner is a keen landscape photographer, and his wife has also been passionately involved in this new stage of the garden.

'Is it possible to discern a person's character from their garden?' Christopher is in no doubt. 'Yes, people's gardens reveal a great deal about them. They leave the psyche exposed. The owner need never have any interest in the garden, directing it from afar or having others tend and control it, but it will after a period of time reflect the owner's character.'

Before we say goodbye, Christopher describes what a garden means to him. 'It's about harnessing nature for one's own benefit. A garden is not a wild landscape but a microcosm of beauty and tranquillity, one hopes; a place where the mind changes gear; a place for restoration and the clearing of thoughts.'

ABOVE: A curving flight of wooden steps complements the sinuous shapes of the cork trees.

RIGHT: A display of contrasts, textures and colours in one of the borders where graceful *Festuca glauca* meets the strict formality of box.

ABOVE: Separating the pool
from the garden, this border
has two aspects. Facing the
pool, *Senecio maritimus* grows
around the lemon trees set on
pedestals of box. *Erigeron
karvinskianus* grows on the
other side of the border.

LEFT: A lookout cabin in the woods exemplifies the blend of nature and culture here. Plumbago grows in the foreground.

OPPOSITE: An orderly stretch of lawn contrasts with the anarchic energy of the cork trees that characterize this garden.

BELOW: Laurel and *Agave attenuata* grow at a fork in the path, with *Lagerstroemia indica* to the right.

EL ALCORNOCAL

WHEN AESTHETICS BECOME ETHICS

Like a religion, or a particular way of living life, the search for beauty is something that brings us closer to the sublime, or divine, and that betters us as human beings. 'The garden teaches you to see things another way, to find beauty in many different forms. I look for beauty in everything, in people, houses, objects and in gardens. I couldn't live in an ugly place,' the owner of El Alcornocal in Andalusia comments, and she goes on to describe how her aesthetic 'has become a way of life, of being'.

The impressive cork trees on the plot were what made the owners choose this place for their house and garden, coupled with the undulating terrain, which adds rhythm and interest. 'When it came to designing the garden I knew exactly what I didn't want. But that wasn't enough – I didn't feel capable of structuring it. For that I decided to hire a professional, and because of my respect for English traditions and skills in this field, I thought it would be interesting to see what an English person could do with this place, and this climate.' After seeing a garden designed by Penelope Hobhouse in a magazine, she immediately knew who she wanted. 'When I met her, I said, "I want mystery in my garden. I don't want to see it all at once. I want it to open out into different gardens."'

'What I like to do is create a really solid structure for the plants and trees to grow into over the course of time, so that the structure is blurred but still discernible,' Penelope explains, adding, 'My taste has changed over the years and these days it's more austere. I prefer designs with straight lines and few plants, but my clients see something I've done before and ask me to repeat myself. However, here at El Alcornocal I had creative freedom and the pleasure of encountering a passionate and sophisticated gardener.' Penelope says that when she first saw the plot she noticed the thickets and the indigenous plants, which had been cut back to reduce the risk of fire. The first thing she decided was to integrate them and use other local plants so that the garden could withstand the long droughts of the region and would connect the house to the surrounding countryside. At the same time, the owner wanted the feel of an English garden.

In making her design, Penelope collaborated with the owner a lot. Speaking about her sources of inspiration, the owner confesses that she visits the garden at Sissinghurst in England every year and was inspired by the White Garden there. However, her chief reference is the land itself. 'One rainy winter a pond formed at the bottom of the garden and this encouraged us to build a pool in the same place, with an artificial stream which pours into it.' But after several years she felt that the garden wanted a more geometric structure, and she ended up designing patterns of box and gravel which offer a striking contrast to the natural and loose style of the rest of the garden.

At the edges of the garden are walls of lentiscs (*Pistacia lentiscus*), rock rose, rosemary and laurel, which imitate the surrounding countryside and separate the house from its neighbours. 'For me the garden is a hiding place,' the owner concludes.

ABOVE: An elliptical pool with water lilies, papyrus and *Gunnera manicata*.

OPPOSITE, ABOVE: Geometric designs in box bring a welcome sense of order and harmony, and an appealing contrast to the wonderfully chaotic shapes of the cork trees (*Quercus suber*).

OPPOSITE, BELOW LEFT: The lawn is mown to different lengths as a simple and elegant way of dividing the garden. Two rows of pomegranates (*Punica granatum*) draw the eye with their bright fruit. In the foreground a splendid *Salvia leucantha* flowers in the autumn.

OPPOSITE, BELOW RIGHT: The shape of this reservoir is in harmony with the house, while also suggesting a traditional drinking trough for animals. In the foreground, sage dances in the breeze.

A magnificent *Wisteria sinensis* frames this view of the garden from the house. Potted herbs and other plants add a homely touch.

THE MEDITERRANEAN

SANTA CLOTILDE

PATHS TO THE SEA

On the Costa Brava the landscape has been modelled for centuries in bold and literally ground-breaking ways by nature itself, as one finds when meeting the Mediterranean tumbling abruptly on to the shore, where pines have turned themselves into defiant, tortuous sculptures as they fight for space and stability. This most beautiful and turbulent of landscapes finds its man-made complement in a garden where solid structure and harmonious visual axes provide a measure of calm.

'My grandfather, the Marquis of Roviralta, was fascinated by the power of the landscape and in the 1920s set about purchasing local estates until he had 45 hectares [110 acres], and then he built Santa Clotilde, the house and garden of his dreams,' explains his grandson Javier Basó. 'He was assisted by the landscape gardener Nicolás Rubió i Tudurí and the architect Domingo Carles. They shifted thousands of tonnes of rocks and imported enormous quantities of topsoil to create the classical garden you see today.'

The aura of the classical Mediterranean world is most forcefully evoked by flights of steps with cypress, ivy and water sculptures, converging in lookouts over the sea. The striking design reveals the influence of Italian gardening, with its structured terraces, classical sculptures and shades of green. Bronze mermaids by Maria Llimona on the main stairway create an aquatic, dreamlike atmosphere as they spout water from their undulating bodies on to passersby. (The 'voyage' under the fine rain between those sirens has to be one of my most blissful moments in a garden.)

At the top of the hill the villa strains towards the sea. In front is a courtyard which serves as a huge anteroom, presided over by four monumental cypresses (*Cupressus macrocarpa*) which are pruned into cylindrical shapes.

Besotted by his creation, the Marquis decided to make his home at Santa Clotilde, to the surprise of his contemporaries. He directed his businesses from here, while keeping an eye on the garden.

'The garden was his great life's work. He involved himself in everything down to the smallest detail. He would pass on his ideas to the designers, and then show the garden staff how to use a rake properly,' explains his grandson, who remembers his grandfather naming him 'the governor' as a child, in order to encourage in him his own love and responsibility for the garden. Such seeds sown by the Marquis of Roviralta among his descendants have borne fruit today in the exquisite care with which they look after Santa Clotilde.

RIGHT: Two bronze mermaids invite the visitor to enter a dreamlike tunnel of cypresses and oleanders filled with moisture and scent, while the enormous shells suggest voyages to far-off lands.

BELOW: A mermaid springs from a sea of *Hedera helix* 'Gracilix' amid a fine spray of water from sprinklers running up the sides of this green stairway.

ABOVE: Four imposing *Cupressus macrocarpa* dominate the esplanade in front of the house.

LEFT: The classical world and Renaissance gardens have inspired the use of different levels in this garden. Here a bust is a focus for light in a green and shady tunnel.

RIGHT: Scrolls of euonymus hedge form two small flat areas in the sloping terrain. *Agapanthus africanus* grows in the foreground.

BELOW: A Roman bust looks out over the Mediterranean from a terrace that still echoes with the gatherings of the intellectuals and artists who met here in the Marquis of Roviralta's day.

LEFT: A sculpture by Fernando Botero is surrounded by parterres of different grasses.

BELOW: Water cascades down through four terraced pools.

RIGHT: The labyrinth of yew with, in the foreground, silver ground-cover plants including teucrium and phlomis.

THE LABYRINTH HOUSE

WINGS OF AN ARCHITECT

The location is almost unreal, like something in a fairy tale. The farmhouse and the garden sit on a hill, looking down to an enchanting village and the Mediterranean beyond.

In this timeless landscape what may be the most daring modern garden in Spain has been taking shape. It is impossible to be indifferent towards it: there is nothing here that is bland or neutral. The architect Oscar Tusquets, working with the gardener Bet Figueras, has let his imagination take flight and spared no expense to realize his dreams. The design shows a desire to draw attention to every feature, from the garden wall to the pool, and displays everywhere an ambition to break with convention and to startle the visitor. The architect has opened the door to another galaxy. Only the little village, which looks as if it is floating on the Mediterranean, reminds you of the real world.

Although there is a sizeable house, to the façade of which extensive modifications have been made, Tusquets has reserved his most imaginative use of space for the garden. 'I've never been interested in taking on the design of a house unless I can also control the garden. At university the great landscape architect Nicolás Rubió i Tudurí taught us that good garden design begins with the

placement of the house. I've always been interested in gardens, and my interest has grown as I've got older. I think it's a passion that belongs to mature people and mature cultures.'

Tusquets has an air of great satisfaction with his work, but although his is a forceful personality he does not hesitate to acknowledge the help he has received from Bet Figueras.

Talking about Spain and what it is to be Spanish, the architect says that he finds the essence of Spain in the mixture of Arab and classical traditions. But, he bursts out, 'I don't want roots, I want wings!' He continues, 'In Spain what we need is shade, and more shade, and always, here and in all places, a dash of mystery.' In this garden he has achieved mystery by creating different spaces with a great deal of surprise.

The bright sunshine lights up the architect's daring games. He puts into words what his work itself is saying. 'A garden is the least useful, least functional, most poetic, most spiritual thing that an architect can make. A garden is a luxury, an excess, a waste of time and money. It's an absurd marvel, a living calendar, a temple . . .' And of course a big influence on those who love it.

ABOVE LEFT: In front of the house, the very different textures and colours of dichondra, cement and water are combined in a radical reinterpretation of the Hispano-Arabic garden.

ABOVE CENTRE: Looking through palm trees (*Phoenix dactylifera*) and cypresses (*Cupressus sempervirens*) to the yew maze below.

FAR RIGHT, TOP: Cement columns, backed by *Agapanthus* 'Alice Gloucester', line the corridor which links the house with the pools.

FAR RIGHT, BOTTOM: The view from the dressing room towards the pools. The container holds a strelitzia.

OVERLEAF: The view from the house over the elegantly spare design composed of lines of water, cement and dichondra.

OASIS IN BARCELONA

TO EACH HIS OWN GARDEN

Few Spanish gardens surprise so much, and so suddenly. This oasis is a breath of fresh air in a polluted, poorly constructed area of Barcelona. It is hard to imagine, but where now anonymous blocks of flats surround this magnificent villa, once there were terraced fruit gardens and a view of distant Barcelona.

The garden's owner, a successful businessman and keen gardener, recounts its history. 'In 1890 my great-grandfather built this Italianate house, and at the same time planned out formal gardens, separated by low brick walls. Each area had its own style: topiary, the Rose Garden, the Orange Grove . . . In 1929 my grandfather had the front of the house redesigned by the Catalan landscape artist N. Rubió i Tudurí, who built a broad terrace with steps on either side above a pool and a collection of classical sculptures.'

The current garden came about when the present owner inherited the estate in 1951. 'I wanted radical changes to the garden. I didn't want a formal layout and for years I had been thinking about a naturalistic garden, with woods and lawns, where smooth organic shapes create an idyllic landscape. For this I had to get rid of the past. For two months, I left the office early in order to devote myself to resculpting the garden, with the help of a digger. I had already pictured the curves in my head.'

The result is a rolling natural landscape, full of movement, whose organic curves contrast with the columns and walls covered with pruned bougainvillea which surround the house, and the elements of the formal layout that remain – the pool, steps, sculptures. 'For me the garden is a canvas on which to improvise – I don't know why I decided to prune the bougainvillea one day, but it's like that because I like it. I don't share the decisions with anyone – the garden is my idea,' says the owner.

'For the boundary between the north and south faces of the garden I went to Ibiza to look for sculptures to line the steps between the two parts. Some olive trees near by were being dug up and I decided to save them, getting hold of nine magnificent specimens, which I planted in my garden. According to the villagers, they're four thousand years old, believe it or not.'

Water is this garden's great treasure. It runs for 5 kilometres/3 miles in a subterranean river from Mount Tibidabo, until arriving here and as if by magic springing from the hill among the moss and lichens. Where once it irrigated the orchards, today it waters a verdant lawn. It goes on to form a curtain in the grotto before ending in a reflective statue pool.

When I ask the owner what the garden means to him he pauses, smiles and answers, 'She's my lover, my beloved.'

LEFT: Trimmed *Bougainvillea glabra* adds a fantastical air to the classical lines of the house.

RIGHT: The immaculate lawn punctuated by the bare trunks of *Phoenix canariensis* finds a surprising counterpoint in the extravagantly coloured plant-covered façade of the house beyond.

ABOVE, FAR LEFT: Softened by bougainvillea, arches below the steps to the main entrance show the influence of Hadrian's Villa. Their graceful lines, reflected in the pool, frame the classical statues that appear to float on the surface.

ABOVE LEFT: Flanking a short series of steps are two imposing olive trees, reputedly thousands of years old. Each measures more than 9 metres/30 feet in circumference and weighs more than 13 tonnes.

BELOW, FAR LEFT: The world through the looking glass. A sunrise lily adds a jaunty note.

BELOW CENTRE: Papyrus grows around the mouth of this grotto, a source of mystery and life in the form of the water that irrigates the garden from a nearby spring. The naturalistic landscaping is the work of the current owner.

BELOW LEFT: A passage below the main entrance to the house allows a view over the pool to the garden beyond, and a chance to appreciate its magnificent combination of the natural with the artificial.

LA TORRE DE CORBERÓ

THE ARTIST'S MIRROR

Breaking the mould with the daring freedom of an artist, the sculptor Xavier Corberó paints and designs this space as though it were an enormous sculpture. Indeed, 'A garden is always a work of art, or it's not a garden at all,' Xavier says emphatically. He has spent more than thirty years shaping this multifaceted space. It covers an entire block of what was formerly a village and is now a dormitory town for Barcelona. A combination of old and new houses is connected by a labyrinthine series of patios to form a thrilling and delightful whole, reflecting the strong and passionate nature of its creator.

At the heart of the collection of buildings is a reinforced concrete tower six storeys high, with a central skylight which the artist himself made seven years ago. 'This place has always been present in my mind, with its octagonal patio and rounded windows – a kind of kaleidoscope. Patios are so integral to my culture that they will always be part of who I am. I've even found myself making sculptures with patios.' Around the tower the patios, as well as terraces, stairways and mirrors, are arranged in a cascade of inspiration that draws on all the arts. The mirrors express Xavier's taste for 'the translucent corner, where the shadows are deep and welcoming'. Standing before the dazzling blue background

of the walls, we see cracked olive trees, flowerpots and sculptures that provoke a storm of sensations.

'When it comes to gardening, my basic approach is the same as the approach I take when I want to improve my mind. Increasing awareness is what I want to achieve, as directly as possible,' he tells me. At the same time he confesses that the garden influences his work in the same way that it does his personality. 'My ideal gardens are like the works of art that inspire me; they heighten my sense of nature. Light, shadow, plants, flowers. Tree trunks and blades of grass. Water, movement, dreams, quietness, peace, curiosity, the passing of time, modest hope. And to achieve that closeness to nature, as for almost anything, you need discipline and determination.

'For me the garden is – as Russell Page wrote – "a song of praise, an act of faith, and the embodiment of hope".' To listen to Xavier, among the mirrors, is to experience an overwhelming sensation of having discovered a new world.

ABOVE: The warm colours of the climbing vine *Parthenocissus tricuspidata* are a beautiful contrast to the cool blue of the wall.

RIGHT: Here the man-made and the natural come together in a composition of contrasting forms and colours. In the foreground are aspidistras, papyrus and anthuriums.

FAR LEFT, ABOVE: On the roof of the tower, pots holding *Magnolia grandiflora*, hydrangeas and *Nerium oleander* form paths around the central skylight.

LEFT, ABOVE: The steps have been planted to create the impression of hanging gardens.

LEFT, BELOW: A group of cacti and other succulents.

ABOVE: Tropical plants in pots are reflected in the mirrors behind.

RIGHT: Glass amplifies the space on this terrace and generates new shapes from the plants they reflect.

BELOW: At the heart of the garden a six-storey octagonal tower forms a kind of kaleidoscope where glass and hanging plants create a fusion between interior and exterior.

XARBET

THE MURMUR OF WATER

I knew the Mallorcan garden of Xarbet long before I met its owner, and I used to wonder how such a classical, ordered, sensual and cerebral garden could be the brainchild of a woman I foolishly assumed to be a carefree, lunching and shopping lady of leisure. I could not have been further from the truth. Today I am sitting opposite her – across the headmistress's desk – and, as you would expect from any good teacher, her description of her garden is clear and precise.

'This place is formed by my childhood memories . . . I was looking for water, and oak trees and mountains on the horizon. This is the agricultural heart of Mallorca. I am very fond of the old, rural part of the island, away from the hustle and bustle; it's peaceful, silent and calm . . . That's what I wanted to create by blending it into the countryside.'

This space explores the origins of the Mallorcan garden, which owe much to the Italian tradition. 'The view was very important when we chose and planned the garden. I wanted to structure it around an axis which would give me my ideal horizon. Once I had that the scale, the layout fell into place. I built a terrace around the house, as the Italians do; the orchard and the mandarin trees are at the bottom . . . I didn't want to be able to see all the garden at once – I wanted it to retain some mystery, for there to be different areas to discover . . . The garden has a very ordered and rectilinear structure with Italian elements such as columns, fountains, terracotta, lemon trees, cypresses, lavender and laurels. The pergolas, however, are very Mallorcan. There are many kinds of climbers, with something always in flower: morning glory, solanum, thunbergia, wisteria and seven types of jasmine, which fill the air with their perfume. Both the pergolas are open to the sun and covered in roses. The pergolas follow the Renaissance style, but form long tunnels which invite one to walk from the house towards the arbours. They appear to be embracing the whole garden in their enormous arms.'

As we pass the nasturtiums spilling on to the path she points out how much she likes to have strongly defined and structured lines 'so that nature can undo them'. She adds, 'The garden gives me a sense of what life is all about, of continuity, of poetry and of the search for meaning. I always remember what I have learned in the garden; how to structure, try things out and take risks.'

OPPOSITE ABOVE: Orange and carob trees line this watery axis which draws the eye to the distant Tramuntana range.

OPPOSITE BELOW: The lemon trees bear fruit all year round, and the bushes of Iceberg roses are in bloom for nearly as long.

BELOW: Detail of lemons and Iceberg roses.

OVERLEAF: This cascading pool is the garden's central element, providing music, movement, reflection and life.

A MEDITERRANEAN GARDEN

Every garden has a story and suggests an adventure. In this one it is the experiences of Heidi Gildemeister, which have significantly contributed to our knowledge of plants which flourish in arid conditions. In her book *Mediterranean Gardens*, Heidi explains, 'When I came to live by the Mediterranean I brought with me memories of the gardens I'd had in other countries – I'm sure other gardeners do the same. In my case these were in Peru and Switzerland. What I pictured here was a tropical jungle; I imagined white flowers against a backdrop of exotic foliage, heavy perfumes filling the air . . . I set about making my dream a reality working all through my first winter here, and in the spring the garden looked fabulous. But as summer wore on, the strong sun scorched the soil and we went for weeks without rain. By the time the lawn had turned brown and there were only 15 centimetres [6 inches] of water left in the tank, I had faced up to reality: the Mediterranean climate was new to me. What kind of plants could cope with such long periods of heat and drought? Where could I find them, how would I choose them and then how should I look after them? How could I save water?'

Heidi has dedicated the last twenty-five years to botanical research and her book. In the book she draws on her experience and wisdom to offer a series of tips on how to develop a Mediterranean garden and create a lush green paradise with a minimum of water.

With her native Swiss precision, she explains each of the lessons the garden has taught her. She says that it is crucial at the outset to have a detailed plan of each area covering the plants and their need for water: such a plan is essential for the efficient use of this precious resource. When I visit, she points out several impressive trees and explains that where there is some shade it is possible to increase significantly the number of plants, as in the protection from the sun that the shade provides a microclimate has been created. The area of the garden given over to lawn has been minimized because of the drought conditions; it now forms just a small carpet next to the house.

Heidi is a founder member of the Mediterranean Garden Society and her research findings and discoveries have given guidance and inspiration to many gardeners in areas that suffer prolonged drought. Her learning is just as valid in places as far afield as California, Chile and South Africa.

One thing Heidi takes particular care about is making sure that in any season there is at least one plant in flower. Having visited the garden on a number of occasions I can vouch for this myself, as there is always some plant or tree whose flower or fruit invites us to look, smell or taste.

Today she can smile with satisfaction at a job well done. She remembers the hostility of the land, the harshness of this climate and how bare were the rocks, now covered by cypresses and a myriad of other plants. She tells me how the magnificent topiary sculptures were once stunted and tangled lentiscs (*Pistacia lentiscus*). As we walk through the shady freshness it is hard to believe how unwelcoming this spot once was.

Heidi looks at her plants with a mother's tenderness as she tells me how she got this plant in a nursery in San Francisco or that one in the Canaries, or another as a gift from a neighbour in the local village. Heidi has travelled far and wide to create a paradise here above the rocks and realize the dream she had twenty-five years ago. Pausing to gaze lovingly around her, she says, 'This garden is all about beauty.'

ABOVE: Drought-resistant lentiscs (*Pistacia lentiscus*) are very well suited to topiary in the Mediterranean climate.

LEFT: This pool, ringed with lentiscs, palms and euphorbias, makes fine use of the terrain.

OPPOSITE ABOVE: Pelargoniums add a dash of colour at the foot of the olive tree.

OPPOSITE BELOW: Hard work has converted a part of this harsh and rocky landscape into a rich and dense garden.

FAR LEFT, ABOVE: Different types of agave with their architectural shapes mark a path through the garden.

LEFT, ABOVE: Plants, rocks and steps combine in perfect harmony.

FAR LEFT, BELOW: This planting may appear entirely natural, but each plant has been carefully placed by the gardener's hand.

LEFT, BELOW: Growing next to the house is a collection of drought-resistant succulents and aromatic plants including American aloes.

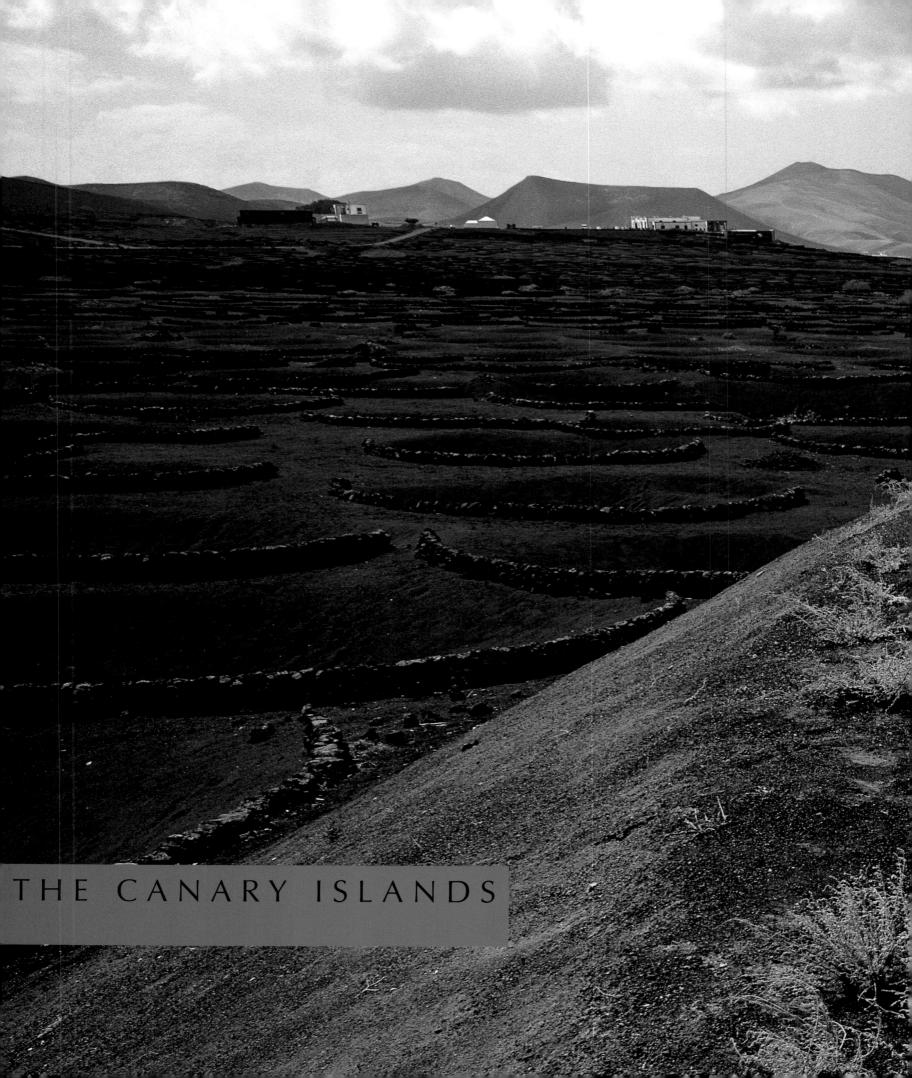

THE CANARY ISLANDS

LA PALATA, TENERIFE

UNDER THE VOLCANO

This tropical garden on the island of Tenerife, surrounded by the fresh green of banana trees, nestles between the foot of the impressive Teide volcano – at over 3,500 metres/11,500 feet the tallest mountain in Spain – and dramatic lava and rock cliffs that plunge into the Atlantic.

Its creator, interior designer Antonio del Real, explains how his adventure began. 'An engineer showed me where all the rocks and different levels were and made a topograph-ical plan of the plot to help me define how the garden would look. I marked out where I wanted to put Mediterranean plants, tropical plants and plants native to the Canaries.'

Before setting to work he thought about it all very carefully, studying the characteristics of each area so as to place every plant according to its needs. 'Closest to the sea I used the hardiest. I put the Mediterranean plants in a sunken area and the tropical plants closest to the house. The tropical ones include lots of lush, exuberant palms.

The edges of the garden are marked by the banana trees, which used to cover the whole plot. In all the spaces I planted fruit trees: avocado, mango and citrus.'

Digging the house's foundations – 'This is volcanic land and my idea when I planned the house was for it to look as though the house had been carried here by helicopter and dropped into an ancient and unspoiled spot' – produced a mountain of enormous rocks and boulders. Perhaps the fact that Antonio was not a native of Tenerife (he was born in Madrid) helped him to appreciate the wildness of this landscape, to see the qualities of a place like this and to understand that the rocks and boulders were its greatest asset. He integrated these into the design, and created pathways that go all around the garden and lead to a viewpoint overlooking the sea.

'The pathways have allowed me to enjoy the whole place. They are uneven and irregular, like the steps and everything else I made in this garden. I wanted to be forced

to go slowly and carefully to make myself contemplate things more calmly. Depending on which way you are facing the paths feel totally different – your spirit and emotions change depending on whether you are going towards or away from the sea.'

But first steps are never easy. 'At the beginning it felt as though the garden would defeat me. I would worry about it all the time and it was far too much work and caused far too many problems. Despite my enthusiasm, I didn't know where to start until a German nurseryman friend gave me something much better than any plant or advice: he gave me encouragement. Now, with time, the garden has settled down and looks after itself. My friend was right when he said, "This could be glorious, but you must continue to fight for it."'

All four elements are here: the water of the sea, the earth of the volcano, the humid, tropical air of the trade winds and the fire always close at hand but deep inside Mount

Teide. All these elements give the place a real intensity.

No one remains untouched by it. 'When they see Palata everyone uses the same word to describe it: "paradise". A friend of mine even says that when he dies he wants to live here,' says Antonio.

'As for me,' he continues, 'I feel more at home in my garden than in my house. If it was up to me, I'd sleep in the garden and would do everything else there too. It's the place where I like to think and find inspiration. I enjoy thinking about how it will end up, picturing the future.' Though he is a respected interior designer, he has no hesitation in making his next statement. 'A garden is real life, a house is just a still life,' he says, smiling.

ABOVE LEFT: Volcanic rocks give the garden depth and character. Pebbles between the paving stones add interest to the design.

ABOVE RIGHT: A watery sitting room in the open air. Cycas and palm trees lend this space a tropical feel.

RIGHT: Further from the house, the garden becomes more jungly.

OPPOSITE: The distinction between indoors and outdoors melts away here. Black pebbles are a unifying element.

BELOW: The massive rocks are a reminder of Teide, the nearby volcano, and provide shelter for the lush vegetation, while the cement path is clearly man-made. *Impatiens* in the foreground and bougainvillea in the background add dashes of colour.

LA CASA BALSA, LANZAROTE

A GARDEN ON THE MOON

I land like an astronaut in this landscape. It is so foreign, magnetic and otherworldly that it startles me like a spasm of life and death, a shock of intoxicating simplicity.

The ground is carpeted by red and black lava that maintains humidity levels in the soil despite the lack of rain. The lava also provides an extraordinarily powerful and abstract backdrop to the cacti and other succulents that take centre stage in the garden like extraterrestrial beings.

Flanked by terraced gardens and patios the house sits in a sunken plot that was once a reservoir, so it is protected from the strong island winds. The former pool is now home to my friend Miguel Cabrera, an ex-Olympic swimmer who has swapped water for lava and competition for gardening. It is called Balsa in honour of the owner's mother. He dedicates the garden to the other mother, with a plaque at the entrance that reads 'To our Mother Nature, who walks in wisdom'.

'I started gardening when, at the age of five, I was mad about pasta, and would slip into the kitchen and steal macaroni and spaghetti to plant them and see them grow. Of course they never did!' Miguel knew as soon as he arrived in Lanzarote that he wanted to create a garden that fitted in with the local style. Once he had created the terraces and patios, he planted cacti and palms in walled beds: their simple shapes blend in well with the minimalist architecture and landscape here. Although cacti (from the

Greek for thorny plant) are originally from the Americas, they have made themselves very at home in the Canary Islands. There are about eight hundred different species of these fascinating plants which can grown to anything between a couple of centimetres and 20 metres/65 feet in height. Their flowers can last from just a few hours to three or four days. Some flower only during the day and others only at night.

'People are surprised when they see my garden and realize how many plants I have. They can't understand why I water them each individually and they are always asking me why I don't get a sprinkler. But I won't because I love that connection between man and nature and the love that each gives the other.' And on the subject of love, Miguel tells a story, laughing, of how his beloved cat got stuck up a very delicate, newly planted tree. All three of them were shaking as Miguel worried for the well-being of his two precious creatures. All three survived!

BELOW LEFT: The torchlike shapes of *Agave attenuata* light up the black volcanic sand, which is used in Lanzarote to cover agricultural land as it holds in the dew and the scarce rain. The house sits in a sunken plot to protect it from the constant wind.

BELOW RIGHT: Various cacti and euphorbias are playfully planted in this sunken patio.

OVERLEAF: There is a dreamlike quality to this garden, where the strong green shapes of the cacti contrast with the black ground.